DELICIOUS DIET COOKBOOK

The Sensible Way to Slim

LOIS LEVINE

MACMILLAN PUBLISHING CO., INC.
New York
COLLIER MACMILLAN PUBLISHERS
London

OTHER BOOKS BY
Lois Levine

The Kids in the Kitchen Cookbook

with Marian Fox Burros

Come for Cocktails, Stay for Supper
The Elegant But Easy Cookbook
Freeze With Ease
The Summertime Cookbook

DELICIOUS DIET COOKBOOK

The Sensible Way to Slim

LOIS LEVINE

MACMILLAN PUBLISHING CO., INC.
New York

COLLIER MACMILLAN PUBLISHERS
London

Macmillan Publishing Co., Inc.
866 Third Avenue, New York, N.Y. 10022
Collier-Macmillan Canada Ltd.

Library of Congress Cataloging in Publication Data

Levine, Lois.
    Delicious diet cookbook.

    1. Low-calorie diet. I. Title.
RM222.2.L43   641.5'63   73-20006
ISBN 0-02-570400-1

First Printing 1974

Printed in the United States of America

Contents

INTRODUCTION: THE SENSIBLE WAY TO SLIM

When addressing women's groups, I try to open up the program for a question and answer session at the end. Inevitably two questions arise. "Why does food have to be fattening to taste good?" and "When are you going to write a diet cookbook?"

After authoring eight delicious but fattening cookbooks, I was hardpressed to answer the first query. But I decided there must be a way and that would lead me to an answer for the second question.

There had to be a way to eat well without weight gain—or, better yet, to eat well and actually lose weight. It has taken a great deal of digging, research, questioning, and, most important, *testing* to find the way. How do you really get slim in a safe, sensible way while eating delicious food? And once you've gotten slim how can you stay that way eating well?

I was pretty sure of the answers from my own experience, but I wanted sound medical advice to back up my ideas. So I did two things. I visited the Yale New Haven Hospital Nutrition Clinic, and I went to see my own physician, Dr. H. Robert Greenhouse. I armed myself with a list of questions: "All the things you've always wanted to know about dieting but were reluctant to ask."

In answer to the basic question, "How can you get thin and stay that way?" Dr. Greenhouse, Mrs. Zehalla, and Mrs. Gardner of Yale all agreed the answer was simple; one word, in fact—calories. The whole subject of weight gain, loss, and maintenance depends upon the relationship between calories consumed and calories expended in exercise and activity. If one expends more calories than he takes in, weight loss will occur. If intake balances output, weight maintenance results. And if you eat more than you use—disaster—you will gain weight. Less than 5 percent of overweight is related to metabolic disorders. If you feel this is the cause of your weight problem, ask your doctor to check. The best diet is one that is restricted in calories but balanced in nutrients. That made sense, but I was surprised to find out that *most* other theories and diet fads not only do not assure weight loss but are potentially dangerous to one's well-being. Reducing diets that have been concocted by a combination of faulty reasoning and wishful thinking can actually produce a state of malnutrition.

Probably the most misleading type of fad diet is one that eliminates a whole category of nutrition while permitting unlimited consumption of another, such as a no-carbohydrate—unlimited-protein diet. The life span of a crash or fad diet is necessarily brief; the dieter, finding he cannot continue, becomes discouraged flitting from one diet to another, each a frustration.

Diets very low in either carbohydrates or protein may at first seem efficient in that they produce some added weight loss for a given amount of caloric deficit, but this transient illusion, depending on the length of time followed, is caused by water loss or changes in water balance. No added loss of fat is actually produced. Sticking to this type of plan is dangerous in reality because it is dieting with inadequate nutrition.

The truth is that a weight-maintenance plan is a life-long proposition and therefore much more important than a short-term diet. After all, many obese people may have been at one time only two or three pounds overweight.

But we aren't really discussing the obese person, the compulsive eater, the poor soul with 50 or more pounds to lose. It isn't that the same facts don't apply, but such a person is going to be hard to convince to try a sensible plan. However, most of us could well afford to take off 5-10 pounds, and once we reach the age of 35 it seems to be a chronic state of affairs. A continuous pattern of gaining and losing larger amounts of weight is not safe, but watching one's weight while still in a 5-10–pound range is not only easy but sensible.

Speaking of the grossly overweight person reminds me that I did ask the doctor if the program for losing weight for an obese person should be any different from that of the 5-10–pound loser. He said that the method is the same—counting calories—but it would obviously take longer to accomplish one's goals. No matter what your goal, a loss of 2-4 pounds per week is the safest rate at which to lose.

I asked whether margarine was less fattening than butter, and about substitutes for sugar or salt. Margarine has the same calories as butter but is lower in cholesterol. I was told it is better to use sugar in limited amounts (remember that it has 13 calories per teaspoonful) than to risk the possible consequence of sugar substitutes. Therefore, there are no recipes in this book requiring sugar substitutes or artificial foods of any kind. Salt, too, is important to the normal healthy body. And here one point must be stressed. Every potential dieter should have a physical examination before beginning a diet plan. The person in good health should try to choose with his physician a reasonable weight goal, depending on his age, metabolism rate, body type, and so on.

My next questions to the experts were about diuretics, diet pills, reducing candies, and the like. The answer to all was a decisive no. But when I asked about a liquid diet food, Dr. Greenhouse surprised me by saying that it could be used to take the place of one meal a day, thereby helping to cut down on calories consumed. However, he stressed that one meal a day would be the safe limit because the body needs roughage to function properly.

Do health foods have anything to do with losing weight? Again the answer was no; only calories count.

My question about taking vitamins when dieting led to another "no" answer. A balanced diet of more than 1,000 calories per day does not need vitamins as a supplement. And speaking of balancing one's diet, it is better to have a little of everything than to cut out an entire category, such as carbohydrates, as mentioned earlier.

Some diet plans allow a list of unlimited foods that may be eaten, as their name suggests, without counting their calories. When the unlimited list contains a substance such as safflower oil, beware. However, our plan too has such a list. It includes black coffee and tea, fat-free broth, bouillon, unflavored gelatin, and sour or dill pickles. Seasonings, spices, lemon juice, and vinegar are limitless and yet add so much flavor appeal to food. Also on this list are most raw vegetables (see List 1). Remember, though, that only raw vegetables are unlimited; if cooked vegetables are eaten they must be limited to one cup per serving. (Cooking vegetables does not actually add calories. It's just that a person is less likely to eat a large amount of raw vegetables. Also, vegetables cook down so that a cup of cooked vegetable is probably more like two cups of raw and then the insignificant amount of calories suddenly starts to mount. Think of carrots, for example, and how many more you could eat cooked than raw.) Water is not only unlimited but recommended, the more the better. So add it to your list.

I wondered out loud if there was in fact such a thing as a genuine craving for sweets. Dr. Greenhouse assured me that there was but at the same time suggested that the quickest way to assuage the craving is by eating fruit. Remember, however, that since fruit is about 40 calories per portion; you cannot use unlimited amounts. Perhaps you can save some fruit from one or two of your meals to use for between-meal sweet cravings. Fruit is the lowest-calorie way to satisfy your craving for sweets.

When I asked if you can stretch or shrink your stomach when feasting or fasting on a diet, the answer once more was no. The appetite center is in the brain, so will power—or, as I choose to think of it, "won't power"—comes from the head, not the stomach. Sometimes the appetite center doesn't tell you when to *stop* eating. Knowing when you've had enough is a learning process that should be started in childhood.

When I asked if age makes a difference in weight control, the answer had to be qualified. What we think of as baby fat will probably be converted through muscle-building proteins as the youngster continues to grow, until about 18. A young child needs more calories as he is growing. An older person's metabolism burns calories more slowly and stores the excess as fat. Therefore he can and should get along with fewer calories each day than a younger person.

So many of us have a habit of snacking between meals and after dinner. This is taboo except for the unlimiteds mentioned and fruit. Our diet allows one citrus and two other fruits per day. These may be taken with meals or saved for snacktime if desired. They must, however, be counted in the total calorie intake for the day.

Liquor is fattening in itself (1 calorie per proof per ounce; i.e., 80 calories for an ounce of 80 proof scotch). When combined with anything other than water or sugar-free soda, even more calories are ingested.

And how many of us can have a drink without a peanut or two? Wine and beer are highly caloric as well. Don't forget that when you count calories you must count everything that passes your lips.

I've heard so much about health spas lately—both resident and "out-patient," so to speak—that I asked about them. Dr. Greenhouse reminded me that exercising in itself will not cause weight loss of any significant amount. For example, you would have to walk about 100 miles to walk off one pound. Of course you could burn about 1,200 calories if you ran 10 miles in one hour, but few of us are in condition for that kind of exercise. A man who weighs 155 pounds must walk approximately 67 minutes, ride a bike for 43 minutes, swim for 31 minutes, or run for 18 minutes to burn up the calories in a single hamburger sandwich. Exercise uses up calories but it can also make you hungrier. The appetite control center in the brain works better with exercise. However, if you exercise without eating additional food, weight loss will occur. Your body doesn't *need* more calories after exercise unless you do heavy work or play football, for example.

Exercising in addition to dieting will produce tighter skin, firmer muscles, and a greater sense of well-being. In other words, this is the perfect combination for a slim shape and the only one that is truly sensible. But again Dr. Greenhouse cautions that your own doctor is the one to determine best how much exercise you can take. One who has been sedentary for many years should not suddenly begin to jog five miles a day, obviously. But after you have your doctor's OK to begin a regular exercise program, you should get right to it.

There is no one time of day best for everyone to exercise. After meals is not good, but any other spot in your schedule is fine. Some prefer first thing in the morning; others, just before bedtime. I find that I can shake the late-afternoon wearies by doing some form of exercise. It doesn't have to be calisthenics; walking, jogging, bike riding, tennis, golf—all are marvelous. The harder you work, the more firmness will result. In a sauna or steam room you will lose water, but as soon as you drink again the apparent weight loss will reappear. I asked about massages and here I was told that the only one to lose weight is the masseur/masseuse who is exerting the physical effort.

Concerning weighing and measuring for results, don't weigh yourself daily, or the ups and downs may give false hope or despair. Pick one specific time, i.e., 8 a.m. Monday morning, and weigh in at that same moment once a week. If you are being faithful you should drop 2-4 pounds easily and keep them off.

Now how should you go about planning this calorie regimen? First of all you must determine—with your doctor—what your ideal weight should be. To maintain weight you can consume 13.65 calories per pound. To lose weight eat only 9.1 calories per pound per day and the excess pounds will disappear. To continue with our mythical figure:

110 pounds $\times$ 13.65 calories = 1,502 calories per day; this will maintain the weight of a 110-pound person.

110 pounds $\times$ 9.1 calories = 1,001 calories per day; this will cause a person weighing over 110 to lose weight.

The following is a typical day's diet totaling 1,023 calories:

BREAKFAST

	Calories
Orange juice (4 oz.), or ½ grapefruit, or ¼ melon	40
Toast, 1 slice	68
Butter, 1 pat	45
Egg, 1 only	73
Coffee or tea	0

LUNCH

Sandwich bread, 2 slices	136
Meat, fish, or cheese, 2 oz.	146
Lettuce, tomato	0
Fruit, 1 piece	40
Beverage	0

DINNER

Meat or fish, 4 oz.	292
Raw salad	0
Cooked vegetable, ½ cup from List 2 or 1 cup from List 1	30
Potato	68
Butter, 1 pat	45
Fruit, 1 piece	40
Beverage	0
TOTAL	**1,023**

As you can see, the diet is most generous in amounts of food and well balanced in relation to protein, carbohydrates, and fats. It even allows a potato and a sandwich with two slices of bread, two items the dieter might easily be able to eliminate. But if you stick exactly to this routine, you would undoubtedly get bored very quickly and then begin to cheat—a fatal error! So the trick is, first, to know how to substitute and, second, to have good recipes for meat, poultry, seafood, and vegetables that are low in calories but delicious to eat so that you can have lots of variety within the confines of the calorie diet plan. We hope to show you both roads to success.

First, let's talk about substituting one food for another. For this a few lists should point the way.*

LIST 1

In this group the vegetables included contain insignificant amounts of carbohydrates or calories. You may eat as many raw vegetables as desired. However, when these vegetables are cooked they should be limited to 1 cup per serving.

Asparagus	Eggplant
Broccoli	Escarole
Brussels sprouts	Greens: beet, chard,
Cabbage	collard, dandelion,
Cauliflower	kale, mustard,
Celery	spinach, turnip
Chicory	Lettuce
Cucumbers	Mushrooms

* These lists were based on the recommendations of the American Diabetes Association and the American Dietetic Association, in cooperation with the Diabetes Branch of the Public Health Service, Department of Health, Education, and Welfare.

Okra

Peppers, green or red

Radishes

Sauerkraut

String beans

Summer squash

Tomatoes

Watercress

LIST 2

Vegetables in this group contain 7 grams of carbo-hydrates, 2 grams of protein, and 36 calories. One serv-ing of ½ cup or 100 grams is adequate. Any vegetable on this list may be substituted for any other in the same amount.

Beets

Carrots

Onions

Peas, green

Pumpkin

Rutabagas

Squash, winter

Turnips

LIST 3

Fruit exchanges here refer to fresh fruit or canned fruits without sugar. A portion as described equals 10 grams of carbohydrates, or 40 calories, and any fruit in the portion suggested may be substituted for any other fruit in its suggested portion as noted on this list.

Apple, 1 small (2″ diam.)

Applesauce, ½ cup

Apricots, fresh, 2 med.

Apricots, dried, 4 halves

Banana, ½ small

Berries, 1 cup

Blueberries, ⅔ cup

Cantaloupe, ¼ (6″ diam.)

Cherries, 10 large

Dates, 2

Figs, fresh, 2 large
Figs, dried, 1 small
Grapefruit, ½ small
Grapefruit juice, ½ cup
Grapes, 12
Grape juice, ¼ cup
Honeydew melon, ⅛ (7")
Mango, ½ small
Orange, 1 small
Orange juice, ½ cup

Papaya, ⅓ med.
Peach, 1 med.
Pear, 1 small
Pineapple, ½ cup
Pineapple juice, ⅓ cup
Plums, 2 med.
Prunes, dried, 2
Raisins, 2 tbsp.
Tangerine, 1 large
Watermelon, 1 cup

LIST 4

The bread exchange list, you will note, contains breads, cereals, starches, and starchy vegetables. Also, sponge cake and ice cream fall into this category. Each item in the size portion noted contains 15 grams of carbohydrates (60 calories) and 2 grams of protein (8 calories) totaling 68 calories, and may be exchanged with any other item on this list, taking note of the size portion allotted.

Bread, 1 slice
   Biscuit or roll, 1 (2" diam.)
   Muffin, 1 (2" diam.)
   Cornbread, 1½" cube
Flour, 2½ tbsp.
Cereal, cooked, ½ cup
Cereal, dry (flakes or puffed), ¾ cup
Rice or grits, cooked, ½ cup
Spaghetti, noodles, etc., ½ cup

Crackers, graham, 2
Crackers, oyster, 20 (½ cup)
Crackers, saltine, 5
Crackers, soda, 3
Crackers, round, 6-8
Vegetables
   Beans (lima, navy, etc.), dry, cooked, ½ cup
   Peas (split peas, etc.), dry, cooked, ½ cup
   Baked beans, no pork, ¼ cup
   Corn, ⅓ cup
   Parsnips, ⅔ cup
   Potatoes, white, baked or boiled, 1 (2″ diam.)
   Potatoes, white, mashed, ½ cup
   Potatoes, sweet, or yams, ¼ cup
Sponge cake, plain, 1½″ cube
Ice cream (omit 2 fat exchanges), ½ cup

LIST 5

This is the meat list, with each item representing 7 grams of protein (28 calories) and 5 grams of fat (45 calories), totaling 73 calories. Note that fish, cheese, eggs, and even peanut butter are also on this list. The last-named item should be limited to one serving per day.

Meat and poultry (beef, lamb, pork, liver, chicken, etc., med. fat), 1 slice (3″ x 2″ x ⅛″)
Cold cuts, 1 slice (4½″ sq., ⅛″ thick)
Frankfurter, 1 (8–9 per lb.)
Codfish, mackerel, etc., 1 slice (2″ x 2″ x 1″)

Salmon, tuna, crab, ¼ cup
Oysters, shrimp, clams, 5 small
Sardines, 3 med.
Cheese, cheddar, American, 1 slice (3½″ x 1½″ x ¼″)
Cheese, cottage, ¼ cup
Egg, 1
Peanut butter, 2 tbsp.

LIST 6

The items on the fat list each contain 5 grams of fat, or 45 calories.

Butter or margarine, 1 tsp.   Mayonnaise, 1 tsp.
Bacon, crisp, 1 slice   Oil or cooking fat, 1 tsp.
Cream, light, 2 tbsp.   Nuts, 6 small
Cream, heavy, 1 tbsp.   Olives, 5 small
Cream cheese, 1 tbsp.   Avocado, ⅛ (4″ diam.)
French dressing, 1 tbsp.

LIST 7

The milk list provides 12 grams of carbohydrates (48 calories), 8 grams of protein (32 calories), 10 grams of fat (90 calories), totaling 170 calories. If the milk is fat free, 2 fat exchanges are allowable. Since fat-free milk essentially contains very little fat, it contains 170 calories minus 90, or 80 calories per 8-ounce portion.

Milk, whole, 1 cup   Milk, powdered, ¼ cup
Milk, evaporated, ½ cup   Buttermilk, 1 cup

As you can see from these lists, food should be measured. A standard 8-ounce measuring cup and a set of measuring spoons will be adequate. Most foods are measured after cooking. Meats should be baked, boiled, or broiled. Do not fry foods unless the fat allowed for the meal is used. It is not necessary to buy or prepare special foods for the one dieter in the family. Everyone can enjoy the same food while the nondieter eats larger portions and can add a fattening dessert if desired. The trick is to eat only those foods on the list in the amounts allowed.

But what do you do about an uncontrollable urge to splurge? It is not only common but very normal. You will be tempted, so you must be prepared for it. When you determine your optimum calorie intake per day, you can quickly figure your week's allowance by multiplying by 7. Keep a small notebook with you in your pocket and write down every calorie you eat. If you go over your limit one day, make up for it the next. It's the total calorie intake for the week that will show on the scale Monday morning. Therefore when the uncontrollable desire for a piece of cake hits, you can eat it, but make an IOU and be sure to pay up in the next day or two by cutting down on that day's allotment of calories.

How did we determine the calorie count of each recipe in this book? First, we compiled our own "Calorie Countdown" (page 137) based on a U.S. Department of Agriculture handbook. The charts are complete and detailed and break down foods into their components and nutrients. By using this calorie count (called Food Energy in the Edible Portion of 1 Pound of Food as Purchased), we rounded the number, in most cases to the nearest factor of 5. I composed my own chart of those ingredients used in the recipes of this book.

The calorie count of wine came from the Wine Institute Home Advisory Service of San Francisco based on a study undertaken by Dr. Maynard Amerine of the Department of Viticulture and Enology and the University of California at Davis.

To count calories of any given recipe I totaled the calories of all the ingredients used and then divided by the number of portions prepared. For example, look at the recipe for French Veal Sauté on page 59.

	Calories
1 pound Italian style veal cutlets	920
1 tablespoon vegetable oil	125
½ pound mushrooms, sliced	60
1 clove garlic, crushed	0
½ cup chopped onion	40
½ cup slivered green pepper	15
1 cup canned tomatoes	50
½ cup dry white wine	13
chopped parsley	0
salt and pepper to taste	0
Total calories	1,223

Since this is to be served in 4 portions, I then divided by 4:

$$1{,}223 \div 4 = 305\tfrac{1}{2} \text{ calories per portion}$$

Naturally, I cannot tell if your veal is fat or lean nor if you use a bit more of one ingredient or another. But following the same method I used, you can calculate almost exactly what calories you will be consuming in each serving of any dish.

A word about the illustrations in this book is in order. It is my contention that looking at pictures of beautiful food will make you hungry. Because you undoubtedly read between meals, that is fatal. Instead, we show pictures here of exercises that you can do to firm up your body. There are simple ones to begin your program. When you feel you've mastered those exercises, go on to the more strenuous ones to work on every part of your figure. A good suggestion: put a peppy, rhythmic record on the phonograph and run through a series to cover each of your flabby areas once a day. Ten or fifteen minutes should do the trick. Repetition plus gradual increase in repetitions should show rapid results.

Now a final word or two. You've made up your mind to do calesthenics and to count calories, and I've promised to help, right? If you were smart enough to buy this book in the first place and to read this far, we can safely assume you are willing to try the recipes. You must read and add first, though—i.e., plan your menus to conform with the daily calorie count your doctor suggests. Then tackle the recipes. None is difficult. Please don't cheat. Your figure won't improve and you'll blame me. My reputation will suffer. So I beg you, stick to your Delicious Diet. Do your exercises every day and smile! You'll be a gorgeous new creature any day.

To Slim Legs *(Easy)*—Sitting with legs spread, lift one leg over the other with big toe leading until toe touches the floor. Repeat with each leg 5 times.

To Strengthen Legs *(Harder)*—With legs spread wide and toes pointed out, bend one knee until you cannot see toes under it. Straighten. Repeat with other leg. Alternate 10 times with each leg.

To Flatten Buttocks *(Easy)*—Lie prone with arms and legs outstretched. Raise right arm and left leg at the same time. Lower, and repeat with left arm and right leg. Repeat 5 times.

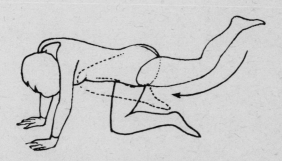

To Flatten Buttocks *(Harder)*—Bring knee to nose, then extend leg back and upward while lifting head. Repeat 10 times with each leg.

To Slim Hips *(Easy)*—Lie flat on your back with left knee bent. Keep shoulders on the floor. Twist right to touch knees on the floor. Repeat with each leg 5 times.

To Slim Hips *(Harder)*—Kneel on all fours. With right knee bent, lift leg to side and then straighten it. Return leg to bent position while sill elevated. Repeat with each leg 10 times.

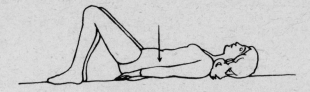

To Strengthen Back *(Easy)*—Press spine flat against floor, count to 10, then release. Repeat 15 times.

To Strengthen Back *(Harder)*—Start on all fours. Let stomach sag, then tighten and arch back. Hold for count of three, then sag. Repeat 10 times.

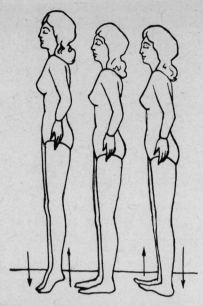

To Slim Feet and Ankles *(Easy)*—Place hands on hips; rise on toes; rock back on heels; lift toes. Repeat 10 times.

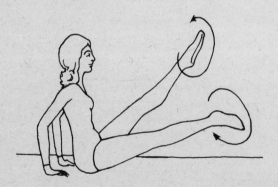

To Slim Feet and Ankles *(Harder)*—Sit on floor, leaning back on hips and palms. Raise legs and make wide circles. Keep heels in, toes pointed out. Repeat 10 times.

To Flatten Stomach *(Easy)*—Sit on floor with knees bent and arms crossed on chest. Roll slowly back until lying on floor. Repeat 10 times.

To Flatten Stomach *(Harder)*—Sit on floor with knees bent, hands behind head, feet held or tucked under a chest of drawers. Slowly raise yourself to a sitting position. Roll back. Repeat 10 times.

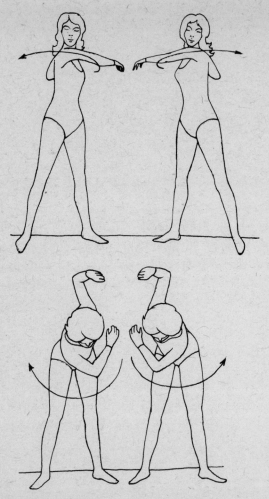

To Slim Waist and Midriff *(Easy)*—Stand with legs spread apart, raising arms and bending elbows at shoulder level. Twist upper body as far as possible to each side 10 times. Then, bending forward from the hips, pretend to hit a punching bag in front of you—without moving your head or hips. Repeat 10 times.

To Slim Waist *(Harder)*—Stand with feet spread apart. Bend over to each side with hand over head pointing to the floor. Repeat on each side 10 times.

To Tighten Arms *(Easy)*—Stand with arms straight out in front of you and touch thumbs. Pull arms back to sides, keeping them at shoulder level. Hold for count of 10. Rest arms at sides. Repeat 10 times.

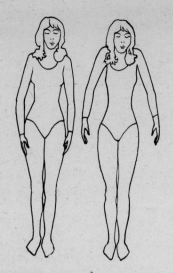

To Relieve Shoulder Tension *(Harder)*—Raise shoulders up to ears, hold for count of 5. Relax. Repeat 10 times.

To Firm Breast *(Easy)*—Stand with feet apart and raise bent arms to shoulder level. Snap elbows back until shoulder blades touch. Repeat 10 times.

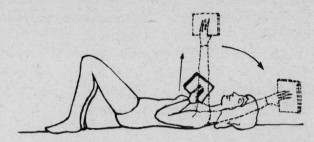

To Firm Breast *(Harder)*—Lie on floor, holding a book in each hand. Stretch arms up so books are above the face, lower arms to sides, then extend overhead. Do not touch the floor. Repeat 10 times.

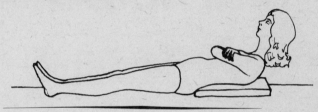

To Firm Chin and Throat—Lie on floor with pillow under shoulders and arms crossed on chest. Raise chin to chest; rest. Repeat 10 times.

To Reduce "Saddlebags"—Lie on side, resting on elbow. With the toe of the upper leg pointing to the floor, raise leg as high as possible. Repeat on each side 10 times.

APPETIZERS AND SOUPS

When this book was first conceived, I thought there would be no hors d'oeuvres, few soups, and no desserts that would fit into my Delicious Diet plan. Let's face it, how delicious can raw celery sticks be? But I did lots of playing around with low-calorie foods and managed to find some really good appetizers that won't wreak havoc with the total weekly count.

I still think you should save the dips and such for entertaining. You don't need them before a regular family dinner. But when guests come it is festive to have a nibble before the meal without using up so many of your allotted calories that you have to skip the entrée. And the hors d'oeuvres recipes here, as is true of every recipe in the book, are so delicious that you need never apologize to guests for the fact that they happen to be low in calories. No one will ever know, but if you do tell you will only receive thanks. Everyone among us is weight conscious, whether dieting or not.

Soup is great for lunch, too—instead of the usual sandwich and salad, for example. Before dinner a simple soup is filling, so these lower calorie soups will take the edge off a voracious appetite and leave less room for too much meat and potatoes.

Party-going and restaurant-dining present certain other hazards. Never go to a party with an empty stomach and your first problem is licked. Arrive late having filled up at home with raw vegetables or bouillon. At a restaurant there's always a dish of celery and carrots to nibble on and usually a clear soup to fill you up. Order a broiled or roasted entrée without sauce and a salad without dressing. By dessert time you should be too full to order anyway. After all, let's be sensible!

So many recipes in the book from appetizers right through to desserts call for plain yogurt that we might as well start out with a simple way to make your own.

HOMEMADE YOGURT

Homemade yogurt is just as tasty as the kind you buy in the store and costs a fraction of the price. If you use a great deal of yogurt in your household I recommend buying an electric yogurt maker, which sells for $10–$12 and removes all the guesswork from the process. However, if you wish to try it on your own it is a relatively simple process. You need 1 quart of skim milk, ⅓ cup dry milk powder, and 1 heaping tablespoon of plain yogurt (bought in the supermarket or taken from a batch previously made). You may also buy yogurt starter at a health-food store.

Place the milk and the dry milk, stirred together, in a pot on the stove and heat until it reaches the boiling point. Cool this down to room temperature, and add the yogurt starter. Place in sterile jars with covers. Wrap the jars with a towel and set on top of the stove for 5–10 hours, then refrigerate. If you buy a yogurt maker, it will include a thermometer, and the electric element will keep the yogurt at the proper temperature for the culture to grow. Whatever method you use, the theory is the same and the mixture must be kept warm and undisturbed to keep the curds and whey from separating. After heating, the yogurt should be chilled for 3–4 hours to allow it to thicken further.

The finished product should be thick and creamy. The acidity can be varied according to your personal taste by varying the length of time in the heating process (longer heating, more acidity). Yogurt will keep in the refrigerator up to a week, but the next starter you take from a batch should be only 3–5 days old. After a month of using successive starters it is best to go back to the supermarket or the health food store for a new strain. Don't forget that in yogurt-making as in most kitchen chores cleanliness is next to you-know-what.

ANGIE'S YOGURT DIP

8 ounces plain yogurt
1 raw cucumber, unpeeled
   and chopped fine

1 clove garlic,
   crushed

Combine all ingredients and let stand several hours to blend flavors. Use as dip for celery, carrot, or zucchini sticks.

Makes 1½ cups (125 calories)
1½ calories per teaspoon (1 dunk)

BAKED MUSHROOM HORS D'OEUVRES

24 fresh mushrooms
   (about 1 pound)
½ cup chopped parsley
1 4-ounce can mushrooms,
   stems and pieces,
   chopped

2 tablespoons minced
   onion
2 tablespoons powdered
   chicken stock base
dash pepper
¼ cup water

Remove stems from mushrooms. Boil caps until tender. Chop stems fine and add to remaining ingredients. Heat mixture in Teflon pan until tender. Remove from heat and stuff into caps. Place on cookie sheet and bake at 375° for 20 minutes.

Makes 24 hors d'oeuvres (7 calories each)

BLUE HEAVEN DIP

1 cup low-fat cottage cheese
1 ounce crumbled blue cheese
1 teaspoon minced green onion
2 tablespoons plain yogurt
1 tablespoon lemon juice
½ teaspoon Worcestershire sauce
2 tablespoons chopped parsley

Blend all ingredients together until smooth. Use as a dip for fresh vegetables, such as celery, green peppers, carrots, or radishes.

Makes 1½ cups (255 calories)
7 calories per teaspoon (1 dunk)

BLUSHING PINK DIP

1 cup low-fat cottage cheese
¼ cup grated Parmesan cheese
2 tablespoons chili sauce
1 tablespoon chopped parsley

Blend all ingredients until smooth. Chill. Serve with cucumber sticks.

Makes 1 cup (255 calories)
7 calories per teaspoon (1 dunk)

COTTAGE DEVILED EGGS

4 eggs, hard cooked
4 tablespoons low-fat
   cottage cheese

salt and pepper
½ teaspoon prepared
   mustard

Split eggs in half lengthwise, remove yolks, and mash yolks with cottage cheese, salt and pepper to taste, and prepared mustard. Heap into whites. Sprinkle with paprika.

Makes 8 (45 calories each)

COTTAGE DIP AND VARIATIONS

½ cup low-fat cottage
   cheese, mashed or
   sieved

½ teaspoon minced onion
1 tablespoon lemon juice
salt and pepper

Combine and blend well. Chill.

For variations, add any of the following:

1. ¼ teaspoon marjoram or 1 teaspoon minced parsley
2. 1 teaspoon celery seed or 1 teaspoon caraway seed
3. 2 tablespoons minced chives or dash garlic salt

None of these variations adds calories, so use as you desire.

2 tablespoons low-fat cottage cheese equals 18 calories
1 teaspoon equals 3 calories

CRABMEAT CANAPÉS

1 7-ounce can crabmeat
1 teaspoon anchovy paste
2 tablespoons grated
  Parmesan cheese

1 tablespoon lemon juice
1 tablespoon mayonnaise
3 large cucumbers

Remove membrane from crabmeat and flake it. Combine crabmeat with next four ingredients. Chill. Peel cucumbers and cut into ½-inch slices. Scoop out center of each slice, leaving thin bottom wall. Fill with crabmeat mixture. Garnish with paprika.

Makes 45 (10 calories each)

DOWN EAST CLAM DUNK

1½ cups low-fat cottage
  cheese
1 7-ounce can minced
  clams, drained
1 teaspoon minced onion

2 teaspoons lemon juice
1 clove garlic, crushed
¼ teaspoon salt
1 tablespoon chopped
  parsley

Combine all and blend well. Chill. Serve with celery sticks.

Makes 2 cups (330 calories)
4½ calories per teaspoon (1 dunk)

GLAMOUR DIP

1 cup low-fat cottage
  cheese
2 tablespoons (2-ounce
  can) minced anchovies
1 tablespoon minced
  onion

1 tablespoon finely
  chopped green pepper
1 teaspoon lemon juice
¼ teaspoon dry mustard

Combine all ingredients and blend. Chill. Serve with carrot sticks.

Makes 1 cup (255 calories)
7 calories per teaspoon (1 dunk)

GREEK DIP

1 clove garlic, crushed
3 walnut meats, grated
1 teaspoon olive oil

½ pint plain yogurt
1 small cucumber, diced
salt and pepper

Combine garlic and nuts with oil to make a smooth paste. Stir into yogurt, add cucumber, season to taste. Chill for several hours to blend flavors. Serve as dip with raw cucumber and zucchini sticks.

Makes 1½ cups (175 calories)
2 calories per teaspoon (1 dunk)

LEMON ARTICHOKES

3 tablespoons minced onion	3 10-ounce packages frozen artichoke hearts
2 small cloves garlic, crushed	4 tablespoons lemon juice
2 cups chicken bouillon	1 teaspoon salt
	¾ teaspoon oregano

Steam onion and garlic in bouillon until tender. Add artichoke hearts, lemon juice, salt, and oregano. Simmer for 5 minutes until tender. Drain, chill, and serve speared with toothpicks.

Makes 3 dozen (9 calories each)

LIVER PATÉ

1 pound chicken livers	½ teaspoon pepper
2 cups chicken bouillon	½ clove garlic, crushed
1 apple, chopped	1 teaspoon minced onion
1 teaspoon salt	

Simmer livers in bouillon for 5 minutes. Drain, reserving ¼ cup bouillon in which livers were cooked. Place livers, apple, and seasonings in blender with reserved ¼ cup bouillon. Blend until smooth. Spread on celery sticks or serve on bed of lettuce and let guests eat with small forks.

Makes 2 cups (25 calories per tablespoon)
Serves 8 for appetizer (90 calories each)

MEXICAN ORANGE DIP

½ pint plain yogurt
2 teaspoons grated
orange rind

¼ teaspoon chili powder
¼ teaspoon sugar

Combine, stir, and serve as dip for raw vegetables such as cauliflower florets.

Makes 1 cup (130 calories)
3½ calories per teaspoon (1 dunk)

MUSHROOM COCKTAIL

2 dozen button
mushrooms
½ cup chili sauce
2 tablespoons catsup
1 tablespoon lime juice

2 teaspoons prepared
horseradish
2 drops hot pepper sauce
½ teaspoon salt
¼ teaspoon pepper

Clean mushrooms and remove stems. Combine remaining ingredients for dipping sauce.

Makes 2 dozen (6 calories each)

PICKLED BEETS

1 1-pound can tiny whole
   beets
½ cup cider vinegar
1 tablespoon sugar
½ teaspoon salt

4 whole cloves
½ small bay leaf
1 small onion, sliced
   wafer thin

Drain beets, reserving liquid. Combine liquid with all remaining ingredients. Bring to boil, then simmer for 10 minutes. Pour over beets and chill at least 24 hours before serving.

Makes 24 (10 calories each)

SKEWERED SCALLOPS

1 pound bay scallops
   (sea scallops halved)
1 pint cherry tomatoes
2 large green peppers,
   cut into 1-inch squares
⅓ cup lemon juice

2 tablespoons honey
2 tablespoons prepared
   mustard
1 tablespoon oil
1½ teaspoons curry
   powder

Alternate scallops, tomatoes, and green pepper on 40 skewers or 3-inch toothpicks. Place kabobs on well-greased broiler pan. Combine remaining ingredients and brush kabobs with this sauce. Broil 4 inches from heat 3–5 minutes. Turn, brush with sauce, broil 3–5 minutes more, basting once.

Makes 40 hors d'oeuvres (20 calories each)

STUFFED MUSHROOMS

2 dozen raw mushrooms
½ cup low-fat cottage
    cheese
1 tablespoon minced
    green onion
1 tablespoon minced
    celery

1 tablespoon minced
    carrot
1 tablespoon minced
    pimiento
1 teaspoon salt
½ teaspoon pepper
1 clove garlic, crushed
2 teaspoons dill weed

Clean mushrooms, remove and chop stems. Combine stems with remaining ingredients. Use to stuff mushroom caps.

Makes 2 dozen (4 calories each)

ZUCCHINI Á LA GRECQUE

1 tablespoon chopped
    parsley
1 teaspoon dried tarragon
pinch thyme
½ teaspoon salt
dash pepper
4 drops hot pepper sauce

1 bay leaf
2 tablespoons lemon
    juice
2 cloves garlic, crushed
1 cup red wine
1 pound zucchini, sliced
    ¼-inch thick

Combine all ingredients except zucchini in saucepan, bring to boil, then add zucchini and simmer 5 minutes. Squash should remain firm. Cool and refrigerate. Drain and serve zucchini speared with toothpicks.

Makes 80 hors d'oeuvres (1¼ calories each)

CLAM CHOWDER

2 cups tomato juice
1 12-ounce can clams with juice
2 tablespoons dried vegetable flakes

2 teaspoons oregano
2 cloves garlic, crushed
2 teaspoons Worcestershire sauce

Simmer all ingredients together for 15 minutes. Serve piping hot.

Serves 6 (45 calories each)

COLD SHRIMP SOUP

½ pound cooked shrimp
1 large cucumber, peeled and diced
1 large tomato, seeded and diced

1 quart buttermilk
salt and pepper to taste
dash hot pepper sauce
2 tablespoons finely cut fresh dill

Mix together all ingredients except dill and blend until smooth in blender. Chill overnight. Serve garnished with dill.

Serves 8 (75 calories each)

EGGDROP SOUP

6 cups chicken broth
½ cup water chestnuts, diced
¼ cup green onions, in ¼-inch pieces
¼ cup watercress, chopped
½ cup bean sprouts
1 egg, beaten

Bring chicken broth to a boil, add water chestnuts, and boil one more minute. Add green onions, watercress, and bean sprouts. Slowly pour in beaten egg, turning off flame immediately. Mix a few times and serve.

Serves 8 (45 calories each)

GAZPACHO

1 cup chopped onion
2 cloves garlic, crushed
1 cup chopped green pepper
2½ cups canned tomatoes
1 teaspoon salt
½ teaspoon pepper
1 tablespoon Worcestershire sauce
1 tablespoon olive oil
⅓ cup wine vinegar

Combine all ingredients in blender. Puree, then chill for several hours before serving.

Serves 6 (50 calories each)

JELLIED MADRILENE

1¼ teaspoons unflavored
   gelatin
1 tablespoon cold water
1 10-ounce can
   consommé
1 10-ounce can chicken
   broth

1 soup can tomato juice
dash Worcestershire
   sauce
⅛ teaspoon salt
1 tablespoon lemon
   juice
lemon slices

Soften gelatin in cold water. Heat together consommé, chicken broth, tomato juice, and Worcestershire sauce. Stir in gelatin to dissolve. Add salt and lemon juice. Chill. Break up slightly with fork and pile into bouillon cups. Top with lemon slices.

Serves 6 (45 calories each)

JELLIED TOMATO BOUILLON

1 envelope unflavored
   gelatin
¼ cup cold water

3 cups tomato juice
2 teaspoons bitters
2 teaspoons lemon juice

Dissolve gelatin in cold water. Bring tomato juice to a boil and add to dissolved gelatin. Cool. Add bitters and lemon juice. Refrigerate at least 3 hours. Break up with a fork and pile lightly into bouillon cups.

Serves 4 (40 calories each)

MUSHROOM VEGETABLE SOUP

2 10-ounce cans chicken broth

2 soup cans water

2 thinly sliced carrots

½ teaspoon ginger

¼ pound fresh mushrooms, sliced

1 tomato, diced

¼ pound fresh spinach, coarsely chopped

2 teaspoons soy sauce

Combine chicken broth, water, carrots, and ginger. Bring to a boil. Simmer, covered, for 10 minutes. Add mushrooms, tomato, and spinach. Simmer 5 minutes more. Stir in soy sauce.

Serves 10 (20 calories each)

SOUP SAUTERNE

1 10-ounce can green pea soup

1 10-ounce can consommé madrilene

½ cup Sauterne wine

dash thyme

Combine soups and wine. Bring to a boil, add thyme. Serve hot with parsley sprig as garnish.

Serves 6 (75 calories each)

TOMATO WINE CONSOMMÉ

1 10-ounce can beef broth	dash onion salt
1 cup tomato juice	dash white pepper
¼ cup Sauterne wine	lemon slices

Heat together beef broth and tomato juice. Add wine and seasoning. Bring to boil and serve at once, floating a lemon slice on each serving.

Serves 4 (30 calories each)

YOGURT SOUP

½ pint plain yogurt	4 cups chicken broth
¼ cup flour	mint leaves

Stir yogurt and flour together in saucepan. Gradually add chicken broth, bring to a boil, and stir over medium heat for 5 minutes. Serve hot or ice cold sprinkled with chopped mint leaves.

Serves 8 (50 calories each)

ENTRÉES:
MEAT, POULTRY, AND SEAFOOD MAIN DISHES

There isn't too much to say about entrées, but there are many recipes here to read about and eventually to eat. Every one of them is delicious and has been home-tested by me and my family. I would like to say a word here about the size of portions. Most of us are overweight; not a lot, maybe, but a little plump. Let's face it; most of us eat too much, especially meat. We not only eat too much *in toto*, but we are guilty of taking too-large portions. For the dieter 4–6 ounces of meat, poultry, or seafood is enough at one dinner meal. The nondieter can stretch it to 8 ounces, no more.

I have a friend who is constantly dieting. She will

often wonder out loud why she has gained a few pounds when all she ate last night was steak and salad. "How much steak?" I ask. "Only a pound," she'll reply. That's 1,020 calories, probably her whole daily allotment of calories, and it doesn't even include the "tiny bit of just oil and vinegar" dressing on the salad—another 100 calories or so.

The object is to finish dinner satisfied but not stuffed. Here, more raw vegetables and less meat will do the trick. Eating slowly as opposed to bolting one's meal will help the dieter gain satisfaction, too. The labor of picking the meat from a lobster adds to one's total pleasure in the meal without adding calories. Good conversation with dinner can add more than a hastily gulped beer, and with no extra calories.

A pretty plate, though it may sound trite, is a great boon to dieting. Planning menus for eye appeal as well as taste is important. Variety of color, texture, and temperature helps a lot. And a sprig of parsley with no calories at all makes a platter look festive, even though it may be a simple low-calorie broiled chicken.

Speaking of chicken, the people at the Yale New Haven Hospital Nutrition Clinic reminded me that skinning your portion of chicken before cooking cuts the calories by one-third. Even if you then rub the piece with a tiny bit of oil, you do not begin to add back what you've subtracted. The chicken recipes here are counted without skin at 155 calories for 4 ounces. Removing the skin cuts out 75–100 calories per serving.

Seafood is low in calories and high in nutrition, and should be included in your diet plan often. It has no cholesterol, either, as does beef, another important factor.

Many of my entrée recipes are made with wine—not a revolutionary idea except for the dieter. But the University of California at Davis has done a study concluding that "when wine is used in cooking, the alcohol vaporizes at a relatively low temperature, leaving only the flavor of the wine to enhance and blend the other food flavors. . . . A dry dinner wine such as Burgundy or Sauterne will lose 85% of its original calories when subjected to a sufficient amount of heat to cause it to lose all its alcohol."

MEAT ENTRÉES

BEEF BURGUNDY

2 pounds beef for stew
1 onion, chopped
1 tablespoon flour
1 cup Burgundy wine
1 10½-ounce can beef bouillon
1 4-ounce can mushrooms, with liquid
2 tablespoons chopped parsley
1 bay leaf, crushed
¼ teaspoon thyme
¼ teaspoon rosemary
¼ teaspoon marjoram
½ teaspoon garlic salt
⅛ teaspoon pepper
pinch cloves
1 pound small white onions, parboiled or canned
1 pound small carrots, parboiled or canned
1 cup celery, sliced

Cut beef into 1-inch cubes. Brown meat in its own fat. Add chopped onion and cook until wilted. Sprinkle flour over meat, stirring until well coated. Add wine, bouillon, mushrooms, parsley, and seasonings. Cover tightly and simmer until meat is almost tender, 1¼–1½ hours. Add onions, carrots, and celery; continue cooking for another ½ hour. Taste and correct seasoning if necessary.

Serves 8 (280 calories each)

BEEF KABOBS WAIKIKI

1 pound round steak, cut 2 inches thick	6 tablespoons soy sauce
1½ teaspoons dry mustard	3 tablespoons lemon juice
¾ teaspoon ginger	1 small eggplant, cubed
⅛ teaspoon pepper	8 whole mushrooms
1 clove garlic, crushed	

Chill steak well or partially freeze. Cut into strips ¼ inch thick. Place steak in shallow pan. Combine mustard, ginger, pepper, and garlic with soy sauce and lemon juice. Pour over steak strips and marinate at least 4 hours. Parboil eggplant cubes 5 minutes, then drain. Thread steak strips on metal skewers alternating with eggplant cubes and mushrooms between folds of beef. Brush with marinade and broil 4 inches from heat, 6–7 minutes on each side.

Serves 4 (260 calories each)

FLANK STEAK

1½ pounds flank steak   freshly ground black pepper
1 tablespoon lemon juice   2 teaspoons Dijon mustard
1 tablespoon soy sauce   ½ teaspoon dried thyme

Rub flank steak with lemon juice and soy sauce and sprinkle with coarsely ground black pepper. Let stand 2–3 hours. Before broiling spread one side with mustard and sprinkle with thyme. Broil 4 minutes, turn, spread second side with mustard and thyme, and finish broiling. Slice on the diagonal, very thin.

Serves 6 (230 calories each)

FLANK STEAK ROSÉ

1½ pounds flank steak   1 teaspoon salt
¾ cup rosé wine   1 teaspoon pepper
10 green onions, chopped   ¼ teaspoon dried
1 clove garlic, crushed   rosemary

Combine all ingredients and pour over flank steak. Marinate 1–2 hours, turning meat several times. Drain, saving marinade. Broil meat 3–4 minutes on each side, basting with marinade, until medium rare. Cut diagonally across grain of meat into thin slices.

Serves 6 (230 calories each)

ORIENTAL MISHMASH

1½ pounds flank steak
1 tablespoon peanut oil
1 package frozen spinach, defrosted
1 package frozen pea pods, defrosted
1 cup chopped green onions
2 cups celery, diagonally cut
½ cup black soy sauce
2 tablespoons Worcestershire sauce
1 clove garlic, crushed
1 tablespoon sugar
1 4-ounce can water chestnuts
1 cup bean sprouts

Cut steak into bite-size pieces and brown meat in oil over medium flame. Add remaining ingredients; cover and simmer for 5 minutes.

Serves 6 (305 calories each)

POT ROAST CHABLIS

3½ pounds sirloin tip
1 clove garlic
seasoned salt
seasoned pepper
½ teaspoon rosemary, crumbled
1 small onion, sliced
⅔ cup Chablis white wine

Rub meat with cut garlic clove, then with salt and pepper, working into meat. Brown meat in dutch oven in fat trimmed from roast, turning to brown well on all sides. Drain off excess fat. Sprinkle meat with rosemary and onion. Pour in wine, cover and bake at 300° until meat is tender, about 2½ hours. Cool pot roast over-

night. Remove fat. Slice meat into gravy. Return to 325°
oven for 45 minutes more.

Serves 8 (235 calories each)

WESTERN SUKIYAKI

1½ pounds lean round or
   flank steak
1 tablespoon peanut oil
½ pound mushrooms,
   sliced
1 small bunch celery,
   sliced

1 bunch green onions,
   sliced
1 tablespoon sugar
¼ cup soy sauce
¼ cup chicken bouillon
3 cups spinach leaves

Cut steak across grain into very thin slices. Heat oil in
heavy skillet and brown meat. Add mushrooms, celery,
green onions, sugar, soy sauce, and chicken bouillon.
Mix well. Simmer, stirring often, about 10 minutes until
vegetables are barely tender. Add spinach leaves and
cook 5 more minutes.

Serves 6 (320 calories each)

MARINATED HAMBURGERS

1 teaspoon salad oil
1½ tablespoons finely
   chopped onion
1 tablespoon catsup
1 tablespoon molasses
¼ cup red wine
1½ teaspoons Worcester-
   shire sauce

1 teaspoon Dijon
   mustard
1 tablespoon sweet
   pickle relish
¼ teaspoon mixed Italian
   herbs
1 pound lean ground
   beef

Heat oil and add onion. Cook until transparent. Add all remaining ingredients except beef. Simmer 15 minutes. Cool. Shape beef into 4 patties. Pour marinade over patties; cover and refrigerate several hours. Broil to desired doneness, basting occasionally with remaining marinade. Takes about 10 minutes.

Serves 4 (260 calories each)

SOPHISTICATED HAMBURGERS

1½ pounds lean ground beef
1½ teaspoons salt
¼ teaspoon pepper
1 tablespoon grated onion
1 teaspoon dried dill weed
½ cup red wine

Mix beef with seasonings and wine. Let stand in refrigerator for an hour or so to blend flavors. Shape into 6 patties and broil, 5 minutes on each side.

Serves 6 (250 calories each)

TERIYAKIS HAWAIIAN

1 20½-ounce can pineapple chunks
2 tablespoons soy sauce
½ teaspoon ground ginger
½ teaspoon sugar
½ teaspoon garlic salt
2 pounds canned ham, cut into 48 1-inch cubes

Drain pineapple and combine syrup with soy sauce, ginger, sugar, and garlic salt. Marinate ham cubes in above syrup for at least 20 minutes. Drain ham and thread on skewers alternately with pineapple chunks, 3 of each to an 8-inch skewer. Cook over coals or broil 4 inches from heat until brown. Baste with marinade. Turn once. Cook about 3–5 minutes on each side.

Serves 8 (235 calories each)

ARMENIAN LAMB

1 tablespoon vegetable oil
1 clove garlic, crushed
½ cup chopped onion
4 cups cubed cooked lamb (1½ pounds)

2 10-ounce packages frozen French style green beans
2 cups canned tomatoes
1 tablespoon Worcestershire sauce
½ teaspoon salt

Heat oil in skillet, sauté onion and garlic until golden. Add lamb and sauté 2 more minutes. Defrost beans, drain, and place over lamb mixture. Combine tomatoes, Worcestershire sauce, and salt. Pour over beans. Cover and simmer over low flame for 15 minutes.

Serves 6 (260 calories each)

GREEK LAMB

2½ pounds lean lamb,
   boned and cubed
salt, pepper
garlic powder
   3 onions, chopped
   1 teaspoon oil
   ½ cup water
   ½ cup white wine

2 tablespoons minced dill
2 tablespoons minced
   parsley
1 bunch celery
3 zucchinis
2 egg yolks
3 tablespoons lemon
   juice

Sprinkle lamb with salt, pepper, and garlic powder. Brown pieces under broiler, turning frequently. Sauté onion in oil. Add water and wine. Put meat into heavy 4-quart saucepan with dill, parsley, and salt. Simmer, covered for 1 hour. Slice celery in 1-inch pieces, leaves and all. Scrub zucchini and slice in 2-inch pieces. Add celery and zucchini to meat. Cover and cook 20 minutes. Beat egg yolks until thick; beat in lemon juice one tablespoon at a time. Gradually stir in one cup of hot liquid from stew. Pour egg mixture over stew and stir into hot sauce until well mixed.

Serves 8 (300 calories each)

LAMB CHOPS IN WINE

4 thick loin lamb chops
1 cup whole tomatoes
1 cup dry red wine

1 teaspoon salt
¼ teaspoon pepper
½ teaspoon dried basil

Brown lamb chops quickly on each side under broiler. Transfer to skillet; add tomatoes, wine, and seasoning. Cover and cook for 10–12 minutes.

Serves 4 (160 calories each)

MINTED LAMB

3 sprigs fresh mint
(1 teaspoon dried)
½ cup dry red wine
¼ cup red wine vinegar
1 clove garlic, crushed

1 teaspoon salt
¼ teaspoon pepper
1½ pounds boned lamb, in
1-inch cubes

Chop mint and combine with wine, vinegar, garlic, salt, and pepper. Pour over lamb and marinate at least one hour. Drain, saving marinade. Thread lamb on skewers and broil about 20 minutes, basting frequently with marinade.

Serves 4 (320 calories each)

PLEASANT VALLEY LAMB

2 pounds cubed, boned
lamb
1 medium onion, sliced
1 stalk celery, diced
1 teaspoon salt
½ teaspoon pepper
2 cloves garlic, crushed

2 cups dry red wine
3 tablespoons tomato
paste
1 cup beef bouillon
1 tablespoon chopped
parsley
¼ teaspoon oregano

In a dutch oven brown lamb on all sides in its own fat. Add onion, celery, salt, pepper, and garlic; cook over medium heat until onion slices are soft. Add 1 cup wine. Cook until wine evaporates. Add tomato paste and bouillon. Cover and simmer 30 minutes, turning often. Add remaining cup of wine, parsley, and oregano and simmer another 30 minutes.

Serves 6 (300 calories each)

CALVES' LIVER SAUTÉ

1½ tablespoons flour
½ teaspoon salt
¼ teaspoon pepper
1 pound calves' liver, thinly sliced

2 tablespoons butter
1 tablespoon lemon juice
1 tablespoon chopped parsley

Combine flour, salt, and pepper. Use mixture to coat liver. Melt butter in skillet and sauté liver over high heat about 2 minutes on each side. Sprinkle with lemon juice and parsley.

Serves 4 (220 calories each)

TONGUE-STUFFED TOMATOES

4 large, ripe, firm tomatoes
4 cups ground, cooked smoked tongue (8 ounces)

1 clove garlic, crushed
1 teaspoon lemon pepper
1 teaspoon grated American cheese

Scoop insides from tomatoes. Turn shells upside down to drain. Dice tomato pieces and combine with tongue, garlic, and lemon pepper. Stuff tongue mixture into tomato shells. Sprinkle with grated cheese. Place tomatoes in shallow pan, pour in water to depth of ½ inch. Bake at 350° for 15 minutes.

Serves 4 (160 calories each)

FLAMENCO VEAL CHOPS

6 loin veal chops
salt
pepper
1 10-ounce can beef
   consommé
2 teaspoons grated
   lemon rind

1 tablespoon Worcester-
   shire sauce
½ cup chopped green
   pepper
½ cup chopped black olives
½ cup chopped onion
¼ cup chopped pimiento
2 tablespoons capers

Sprinkle chops with salt and pepper. Brown on both sides under broiler. Transfer chops to skillet; add all remaining ingredients. Cover and simmer 40–45 minutes or until meat is tender.

Serves 6 (200 calories each)

FRENCH VEAL SAUTÉ

1 pound Italian style veal
cutlets
1 tablespoon vegetable oil
½ pound mushrooms,
sliced
1 clove garlic, crushed
½ cup chopped onion

½ cup slivered green
pepper
1 cup canned tomatoes
½ cup dry white wine
chopped parsley
salt and pepper to taste

Cut veal into 1-inch squares. Brown it in vegetable oil. Remove veal from pan and in same pan brown mushrooms, garlic, and onions. Add peppers, tomatoes, and wine. Return meat to pan. Cover and simmer 30 minutes. Sprinkle with parsley, salt, and pepper.

Serves 4 (305 calories each)

VEAL AND CHICKEN SALAD

1 cup cooked veal, cut in
strips
1 cup cooked chicken,
diced
½ cup sliced celery
2 apples, diced

6 stuffed olives, sliced
1 tablespoon mayonnaise
1 tablespoon plain yogurt
1 tablespoon catsup
1 tablespoon minced
chives

Combine veal and chicken with celery, apples, and olives. In separate bowl combine mayonnaise, yogurt, catsup, and chives to make dressing. Toss dressing with veal-chicken combination. Chill. Serve on lettuce leaves.

Serves 6 (125 calories each)

VEAL MARSALA

1 pound Italian style veal
  cutlets
2 tablespoons flour
1 teaspoon salt

dash pepper
1½ tablespoons butter
½ cup dry Marsala wine

Pound veal until very thin. Dredge each slice with mixture of flour, salt, and pepper. Melt butter in large skillet over medium heat. Cook veal about one minute on each side. Remove veal as it browns. Then return all veal to pan with Marsala. Cook, scraping bottom of skillet until gravy thickens slightly—about 2–3 minutes.

Serves 4 (280 calories each)

POULTRY ENTRÉES

CASSEROLE BAKED CHICKEN

1 fryer (2 pounds), cut up,
skin removed
1 cup canned tomatoes,
with liquid
½ cup white wine

1 clove garlic, crushed
¼ cup minced parsley
¼ teaspoon basil
¼ teaspoon rosemary

Combine all ingredients and pour over chicken in shallow pan. Bake uncovered at 325° for 1½ hours. Baste frequently.

Serves 4 (170 calories each)

CHICKEN CACCIATORE

2 fryers (1½ pounds each), skin removed
2 cups water
2 8-ounce cans tomato sauce
1 teaspoon oregano
½ cup dry white wine
½ cup chopped onion
1 green pepper, diced
1 clove garlic, crushed
½ teaspoon salt
¼ teaspoon pepper

Simmer chicken in water in covered saucepan for 30 minutes. Cool. Remove meat from bones. Skim fat from stock. Combine chicken, 2 cups stock, and remaining ingredients in covered saucepan. Simmer 20 minutes. Uncover pan and simmer 10 minutes more.

Serves 8 (185 calories each)

CHICKEN CURRY

2 broilers, cut in serving pieces, skin removed
½ cup chopped green onions
1 clove garlic, crushed
1 cup plain yogurt
2 cups water
1 teaspoon ground ginger
1 teaspoon curry powder
1 green pepper, chopped
2 whole cardamoms
1 stick cinnamon
½ teaspoon salt
¼ teaspoon pepper

Brown chicken pieces on all sides under broiler. Remove to a dutch oven. Cover chicken with onions, garlic, yogurt, water, ginger, and curry powder. Cover and simmer for 15 minutes. Add green pepper, cardamoms, cinnamon, salt, and pepper; simmer 20 minutes more or until chicken is tender.

Serves 8 (175 calories each)

CHICKEN ORIENTALE

2 fryers, cut up, skin
   removed
1 16-ounce can pineapple
   chunks, unsweetened
3 tablespoons wine
   vinegar

1 tablespoon soy sauce
½ teaspoon dry mustard
1 teaspoon salt
¼ teaspoon pepper
1 green pepper, cut in
   strips

Place chicken, skin side up, in shallow baking dish in single layer. Cover with pineapple chunks. Combine juice from pineapple with vinegar, soy sauce, mustard, salt, and pepper. Pour over chicken and bake at 325° for 50 minutes, basting occasionally. Add pepper strips and bake 15 minutes more.

Serves 8 (180 calories each)

CHICKEN TARRAGON

1 fryer (2 pounds),
   quartered, skin removed
1 teaspoon seasoned salt
½ teaspoon lemon pepper
½ cup chicken bouillon

1 tablespoon fresh
   tarragon, chopped
¼ cup lemon juice
3 green onions, minced

Sprinkle chicken with salt and lemon pepper. Brown on all sides under broiler. Transfer chicken to skillet. Combine all remaining ingredients and pour over chicken. Cover skillet and simmer 20 minutes.

Serves 4 (165 calories each)

CHICKEN WITH MUSHROOMS AND WINE

1 broiler, cut into serving
  pieces, skin removed
salt
pepper
garlic powder

¼ pound mushrooms,
  sliced
3 tablespoons tarragon
¾ cup dry white wine

Sprinkle chicken pieces with salt, pepper, and garlic powder. Brown under broiler, turning. Put chicken and sliced mushrooms into casserole. Sprinkle with tarragon. Pour wine over chicken. Cover casserole and bake at 350° for 1½ hours.

Serves 4 (170 calories each)

CHINESE CHICKEN

4 chicken breasts, skinned
  and boned
1 tablespoon vegetable oil
¼ cup sliced celery
¼ cup bamboo shoots,
  diced
¼ cup sliced water
  chestnuts

¼ cup bean sprouts
1 7-ounce package frozen
  pea pods, defrosted, or
  ½ pound fresh
1 tablespoon soy sauce
1 cup chicken bouillon
1 tablespoon cornstarch
2 tablespoons cold water

Cut chicken into uniform strips and sauté in oil quickly over high heat. Add vegetables, soy sauce, and bouillon. Cover and simmer for 5 minutes. Combine cornstarch and cold water and stir into chicken and vegetables until thickened.

Serves 4 (250 calories each)

COQ AU VIN

1 broiler, cut up, skin removed
1 cup chopped onion
1 clove garlic, crushed
½ pound fresh mushrooms, sliced
1½ cups dry red wine
1 teaspoon salt
1 teaspoon tarragon
1 bay leaf

Brown chicken pieces on all sides under broiler. Place chicken in casserole. In drippings from broiler pan, sauté onion, garlic, and mushrooms. Stir in wine, salt, tarragon, and bay leaf. Heat to boiling, then pour over chicken. Cover casserole and bake at 350° for 30–40 minutes.

Serves 4 (205 calories each)

FAR EAST CHICKEN

2 fryers, quartered, skin removed
1 onion, chopped
1 tablespoon Worcestershire sauce
1 teaspoon curry powder
½ teaspoon ground ginger
½ teaspoon garlic salt
2 cups chicken stock
16 small white onions, peeled
6 carrots, peeled and sliced
16 whole fresh mushrooms
2 tablespoons chopped parsley
1 tablespoon shredded coconut

Brown chicken on all sides under broiler. Transfer chicken to dutch oven. Add remaining ingredients except coconut, cover, and simmer 45 minutes. Sprinkle with coconut when ready to serve.

Serves 8 (240 calories each)

GOLD DUST CHICKEN

1 fryer (2 pounds),
    quartered, skin removed
½ teaspoon curry powder
½ teaspoon dry mustard
1 tablespoon honey
½ teaspoon grated orange
    rind

½ cup orange juice
½ teaspoon salt
dash pepper
2 oranges, peeled and
    sliced
parsley

Sprinkle chicken with curry powder and mustard, rub well into flesh. Place in shallow pan, skin side up. Combine honey, orange rind, juice, salt, and pepper. Pour over chicken. Cover with foil and bake at 325° for 2 hours, basting frequently. Garnish with orange slices and parsley.

Serves 4 (215 calories each)

HERBED CHICKEN LIVERS

1 tablespoon dry mustard
1 teaspoon curry powder
1 tablespoon ground
    ginger
1 tablespoon garlic
    powder

1 tablespoon coarse salt
1 pound chicken livers
1 tablespoon olive oil
½ cup chicken bouillon
3 tablespoons chopped
    parsley

Mix together all seasonings and place in plastic bag with livers. Shake to coat thoroughly. Heat oil in skillet and sauté livers until browned, turning frequently. Pour bouillon over livers and simmer 5 minutes. Sprinkle with chopped parsley.

Serves 4 (180 calories each)

HONEY DRUMSTICKS

4 chicken legs with thighs
1 teaspoon salt
¼ teaspoon pepper
¼ cup orange juice

1 tablespoon honey
1 teaspoon Worcester-
   shire sauce
¼ teaspoon dry mustard

Place chicken, skin side up, in shallow baking dish. Sprinkle with salt and pepper. Bake at 375° for 30 minutes. Combine remaining ingredients and brush over drumsticks. Bake and baste for 20 minutes more.

Serves 4 (215 calories each)

ITALIAN CHICKEN

1 fryer (2 pounds),
   quartered, skin removed
seasoned salt and pepper
1 large onion, chopped
1 1-pound can whole
   tomatoes
1 8-ounce can tomato
   sauce
½ cup dry white wine

1 teaspoon salt
¼ teaspoon pepper
½ bay leaf
⅛ teaspoon thyme
¼ teaspoon marjoram
1 clove garlic, crushed
4 medium zucchinis,
   sliced ½ inch thick

Sprinkle chicken with salt and pepper. Brown on all sides under broiler. Transfer to casserole. Combine remaining ingredients and pour over chicken. Cover casserole and bake at 350° for 1½ hours.

Serves 4 (220 calories each)

LEMON CHICKEN WITH TARRAGON SAUCE

LEMON CHICKEN

½ cup lemon juice
4 chicken breasts, boned and skin removed

1 teaspoon salt
freshly ground pepper

Squeeze lemon juice over chicken and let stand at room temperature for 15 minutes. Season with salt and pepper. Broil 20–25 minutes, turning and basting with lemon juice and pan drippings.

TARRAGON SAUCE

½ pound thinly sliced mushrooms
½ cup chicken bouillon

½ teaspoon dried tarragon
salt
pepper

Simmer mushrooms in bouillon until tender, about 10 minutes. Add seasonings and pour over chicken breasts.

Serves 4 (185 calories each)

ORANGE CHICKEN

1 fryer (2 pounds), quartered, skin removed
1 teaspoon basil
1 tablespoon orange rind

3 tablespoons orange juice
3 tablespoons lemon juice
½ cup ginger ale

Rub chicken with basil and grated orange rind. Brown on all sides under broiler, basting with remaining ingredients combined. This will take about 15 minutes.

Then cover with foil and bake at 400° for 30 minutes more, basting frequently.

Serves 4 (180 calories each)

ORIENTAL CHICKEN SALAD

2 envelopes unflavored gelatin

½ cup cold water

2 cups chicken bouillon, boiling hot

½ teaspoon ground ginger

2 tablespoons soy sauce

1 teaspoon sugar

½ teaspoon garlic salt

2½ cups crushed pineapple, with juice (20-ounce can)*

2 cups cooked chicken, cubed (4 half breasts)

1 cup diced celery

2 tablespoons chopped cucumber

Soak gelatin in cold water to soften, then dissolve in hot bouillon. Stir in ginger, soy sauce, sugar, and garlic salt. Add remaining ingredients. Pour into 2-quart mold and chill until firm. Remove from mold to serve.

Serves 8 (140 calories each)

* Canned pineapple is available in its own juice with no sugar, and therefore no calories, added.

SHERRIED LEMON CHICKEN

¾ cup dry sherry
1 lemon
1 teaspoon salt

1 2-pound frying chicken,
cut up, skin removed

Combine sherry, juice of half lemon, salt. Pour over chicken to marinate for 2 hours. Remove chicken, saving marinade. Brown chicken on all sides under broiler. Place chicken in dutch oven. Pour marinade and other half lemon cut into thin slices over chicken. Cover. Simmer on top of stove for 30 minutes or until tender.

Serves 4 (170 calories each)

SWEET AND SOUR CHICKEN

1 fryer (2 pounds), cut-up,
skin removed
½ cup wine vinegar
½ cup soy sauce
2 cloves garlic, crushed
salt and pepper to taste

1 teaspoon prepared
mustard
¼ cup catsup
2 tablespoons honey
½ cup chicken bouillon

Place chicken parts in 2-quart casserole and cover with sauce made of remaining ingredients. Cover and bake at 325° for 1½ hours or until tender.

Serves 4 (220 calories each)

SEAFOOD ENTRÉES

CRABMEAT CASSEROLE

1 10-ounce package frozen cauliflower

1 10-ounce package frozen spinach

1 chicken bouillon cube

½ cup water

1 teaspoon minced onion

⅓ cup instant non-fat dry milk powder

salt and pepper to taste

2 7-ounce cans crabmeat

1 tablespoon grated Parmesan cheese

paprika

Cook cauliflower and spinach as directed on their packages and drain well. Combine cauliflower, bouillon, water, onion, milk powder, salt, and pepper in blender and blend until smooth. Combine with spinach and crab-meat in 1-quart casserole. Sprinkle with cheese and paprika. Bake at 375° for 12–15 minutes or until golden.

Serves 4 (145 calories each)

TOMATOES STUFFED WITH CRABMEAT

8 large tomatoes
1 teaspoon salt
dash pepper
12 ounces frozen crabmeat
1 tablespoon lemon juice
grated rind of half lemon

2 tablespoons minced chives
2 tablespoons chopped parsley
1 tablespoon grated cheese

Wash tomatoes, remove stem ends and centers; sprin-kle shells with salt and pepper. Dice centers of toma-toes and combine with crabmeat, lemon juice and rind, chives, and parsley. Place in tomatoes. Sprinkle with grated cheese. Bake at 350° for 20-25 minutes until tomatoes are tender.

Serves 8 (65 calories each)

BAKED FISH FILLETS

1½ pounds fish fillets
  (flounder, sole, etc.)
salt
pepper
  1 cup plain yogurt
  2 tablespoons chopped
    dill pickle
  2 tablespoons minced
    onion

2 tablespoons chopped
  green pepper
1 tablespoon chopped
  parsley
1 tablespoon lemon juice
¼ teaspoon dry mustard
paprika

Arrange fish in baking dish. Sprinkle with salt and pepper. Combine remaining ingredients except paprika and spread over fish. Sprinkle with paprika. Bake at 375° for 20 minutes.

Serves 6 (90 calories each)

BROILED FISH WITH WHITE WINE

2 pounds fish (slices,
  fillets, or whole)
salt
pepper
1 tablespoon lemon juice

1 onion, sliced thin
1 tablespoon butter
¼ teaspoon paprika
¾ cup white wine
3 stuffed olives

Place fish in foil-lined shallow pan; whole fish should be split lengthwise and placed skin side down. Sprinkle fish with salt, pepper, and lemon juice; top with onion slices. Dot with butter and sprinkle with paprika. Place under broiler. When butter starts to melt begin basting with wine. Broil, basting, until fish flakes easily when tested with fork. Remove fish to hot platter, garnish with sliced olives.

Serves 6 (145 calories each)

FILLETS OF SOLE VERONIQUE

2 pounds fillets of sole	1½ pounds seedless grapes
1 cup dry white wine	salt
	pepper

Marinate fish for 30 minutes in wine. Cut grapes in half and spread on foil-lined baking pan. Place fish on grapes and pour wine over. Bake at 350° for 20 minutes, basting once or twice. Salt and pepper to taste after cooking.

Serves 8 (140 calories each)

FLOUNDER FILLETS

1½ pounds flounder fillets	1 tablespoon chopped chives
1 tablespoon melted butter	1 teaspoon paprika
2 tablespoons lemon juice	salt
1 tablespoon grated lemon rind	pepper

Place fillets on foil-lined baking pan. Combine remaining ingredients and pour over fish. Bake at 350° for 20 minutes. Put pan under broiler, about 3 inches from heat, and broil 2–3 minutes.

Serves 6 (105 calories each)

FLOUNDER ROLLS

1 pound fresh spinach	1 tablespoon grated onion
1 egg	1 clove garlic, crushed
½ teaspoon nutmeg	4 large flounder fillets
1 teaspoon salt	(1 pound)
¼ teaspoon pepper	4 slices tomato

Cook spinach and drain well. Combine spinach with egg and seasonings. Spread spinach mixture on flounder fillets. Roll each as for jelly roll. Secure with toothpicks. Set on end in a baking dish. Top each roll with a slice of tomato. Bake at 350° for 20 minutes.

Serves 4 (145 calories each)

ORIENTAL FISH

1½ pounds fish fillets	¼ teaspoon salt
1½ tablespoons soy sauce	¼ teaspoon ground ginger
⅛ teaspoon ground cinnamon	½ teaspoon grated lemon rind

Wipe fish with damp cloth. Place on foil-lined pan. Combine all ingredients and pour over fish. Bake at 325° for 25 minutes.

Serves 6 (90 calories each)

SOLE CASTELLANA

6 green onions, chopped
½ pound mushrooms,
   chopped
1 pound fillets of sole
1 tablespoon soy sauce
salt

pepper
½ cup orange juice
½ cup white wine
2 tablespoons grated
   orange rind

Arrange half of green onions and mushrooms in baking dish. Place fish on top. Brush fillets with soy sauce. Cover with remaining onions and mushrooms. Sprinkle with salt and pepper. Combine orange juice, wine, and orange rind and pour over fish. Bake at 350° for 15 minutes.

Serves 4 (140 calories each)

BAKED HALIBUT STEAK

1 tablespoon butter
4 tablespoons chopped
   onion
4 tablespoons chopped
   parsley
salt

pepper
2 pounds halibut steak, cut
   1½ inches thick
1 egg yolk
1 teaspoon bitters
lemon wedges

With part of butter, grease a baking pan. Sprinkle with half the onion and parsley, salt, and pepper to taste. Lay halibut steak on top and brush fish with egg yolk. Sprinkle with salt, pepper, and remaining onion and parsley. Pour bitters over all and dot with remaining butter. Bake at 400° for 20 minutes. Serve with lemon wedges.

Serves 6 (180 calories each)

RITZY FISH SALAD

½ cup plain yogurt   capers
½ cup chili sauce   lettuce
 4 cups cooked white fish   pimiento
   (halibut, haddock, etc.)

Blend yogurt and chili sauce. Toss gently with flaked fish. Season with capers. Serve on lettuce leaves garnished with pimiento.

Serves 6 (140 calories each)

SHERRY BAKED FISH

2 pounds (1 thick slice)   1 lemon, very thinly sliced
halibut, sea bass, etc.   2 8-ounce cans tomato
salt   sauce
pepper   ½ cup sherry
1 medium onion, very   2 tablespoons melted
  thinly sliced   butter

Place fish in oven-proof dish. Sprinkle with salt and pepper; arrange onion and lemon slices on top. Mix tomato sauce, sherry, and melted butter; pour over fish.

Bake at 325° for 20-30 minutes or until fish flakes when tested with fork.

Serves 8 (165 calories each)

LOBSTER GRAPEFRUIT CUP

1 tablespoon olive oil
1 tablespoon tarragon vinegar
½ teaspoon salt
1 tablespoon prepared mustard
½ teaspoon horseradish
1 teaspoon paprika
1 tablespoon minced green onion

¼ cup finely minced celery
1 tablespoon minced chives
2 tablespoons chopped parsley
2 fresh grapefruits
12 ounces diced, cooked lobster meat

Beat together oil, vinegar, and salt. Add mustard, horseradish, paprika, onion, celery, chives, and parsley. Blend thoroughly. Cut grapefruit in half; cut around sections. Remove fruit, discard all membranes. Mix grapefruit sections with lobster and sauce. Toss well. Fill grapefruit halves with mixture and serve well chilled.

Serves 4 (150 calories each)

OYSTER STEW

1 pint fresh shelled
oysters
12 ounces clam juice
½ teaspoon salt
¼ teaspoon white pepper
¼ teaspoon celery salt

2 cups skimmed milk
1 tablespoon butter
1 teaspoon Worcester-
shire sauce
4 ounces water chestnuts,
diced

Combine oysters and clam juice in top of double boiler. Heat but do not boil. Add salt, pepper, and celery salt. Add, but do not boil, milk, butter, and Worcestershire sauce. When hot, serve with water chestnuts in soup bowls. The water chestnuts serve as "crunch" in place of more caloric oyster crackers.

Serves 4 (180 calories each)

LEMON SAUCED SALMON

½ cup dry white wine
½ cup water
¼ teaspoon dill weed
½ teaspoon mustard seed
1 lemon, thinly sliced

1 tablespoon butter
4 fresh salmon steaks
(1 pound)
2 teaspoons cornstarch
1 tablespoon water

Combine wine, water, dill, mustard, lemon, and butter in a large skillet; heat to boiling. Add salmon steaks, cover and simmer 15 minutes or until fish flakes easily with a fork. Remove fish to heated platter. Stir cornstarch into 1 tablespoon water; blend into pan juices and stir until mixture thickens. Spoon over fish to serve.

Serves 4 (198 calories each)

SALMON IN CIDER

4 salmon steaks

4 teaspoons prepared
mustard

1 tablespoon butter

¼ cup cider

Spread salmon steaks with mustard. Melt butter in skillet; add cider. Sauté salmon in cider-butter mixture for 10 minutes on each side.

Serves 4 (200 calories each)

BROILED CURRIED SCALLOPS

2 tablespoons honey

1 teaspoon curry powder

2 tablespoons prepared
mustard

½ teaspoon lemon juice

1½ pounds bay scallops

Mix together honey, curry powder, mustard, and lemon juice. Arrange scallops in foil-lined broiler pan. Brush scallops generously with curry sauce. Place pan under broiler in furthest position from source of heat. Broil 10–12 minutes, turning and basting frequently.

Serves 4 (170 calories each)

SCALLOPS

1 tablespoon butter

1 teaspoon Worcestershire
sauce

¼ cup minced onion

½ cup white wine

1 pound bay scallops

Melt butter with Worcestershire sauce. Add onion and cook until golden. Combine with white wine and pour over scallops. Bake at 500° for 10 minutes.

Serves 4 (95 calories each)

SCALLOPS PROVENÇALE

¾ cup water
1 stalk celery
½ onion
½ carrot
¼ lemon, sliced
2 sprigs parsley
5 peppercorns
1 small bay leaf
pinch thyme
1 teaspoon salt
1 pound bay scallops

½ pound mushrooms, sliced
1 tablespoon butter
½ pound zucchini, thinly sliced
½ bunch parsley, chopped fine
2 cloves garlic, crushed
salt and pepper to taste
1 tablespoon lemon juice

Combine first 10 ingredients and simmer for 20 minutes. In this mixture simmer scallops for 5–8 minutes. In skillet sauté mushrooms in butter. Boil zucchini separately for 2 minutes and drain. Drain scallops and pat dry. Add them to skillet with mushrooms, zucchini, and remaining ingredients. Heat to serve.

Serves 4 (120 calories each)

BOB'S SHRIMP

1 tablespoon vegetable oil
1 onion, chopped
1 clove garlic, crushed
3 tablespoons chopped green pepper
2 tablespoons chopped parsley
½ cup tomato juice
1 8-ounce can stewed tomatoes (or 2 medium tomatoes)
½ teaspoon salt
½ teaspoon basil
dash pepper
1 pound raw shrimp, peeled

Heat oil; add onions, garlic, pepper, and parsley. Sauté until onion is golden; add tomatoes, tomato juice, and remaining seasonings. Cook until tomatoes are soft, then add shrimp. Cook, covered, for 10 minutes.

Serves 4 (165 calories each)

EGGS FOO YONG

5 eggs
½ cup water
¼ cup green onions, slivered
½ cup bean sprouts
½ pound cooked shrimp, chopped
½ pound crabmeat
½ cup water chestnuts, sliced
½ cup mushrooms, sliced
½ teaspoon salt
¼ teaspoon pepper
2 teaspoons soy sauce
1 tablespoon butter

Beat eggs with water. Add remaining ingredients except butter. Melt butter in large frying pan. Pour in egg mixture and brown on both sides, pancake style. Cut into wedges to serve.

Serves 6 (175 calories each)

HAWAIIAN SHRIMP MOLD

2 envelopes unflavored
gelatin
1 12-ounce can vegetable
juice cocktail
1 12-ounce can pineapple
juice
½ teaspoon seasoned salt
¼ teaspoon thyme

1 tablespoon chopped
chives
3 drops hot pepper sauce
⅓ cup water
2½ tablespoons lemon
juice
1 pound cooked shrimp,
diced

Soften gelatin in vegetable juice. Heat to dissolve. Remove from heat; blend in pineapple juice, salt, thyme, chives, hot pepper sauce, water, and lemon juice. Chill until consistency of unbeaten egg whites. Fold in shrimp. Pour into 1½-quart mold and chill until firm. Unmold and serve on lettuce leaves.

Serves 8 (95 calories each)

SHRIMP SALAD

2 4-ounce cans tiny shrimp
1 cup low-fat cottage
cheese
2 tablespoons lemon juice
4 water chestnuts, diced
2 green onions, sliced

4 tablespoons diced green
pepper
salt
pepper
1 clove garlic, crushed

Combine all ingredients and let stand at least 30 minutes to blend flavors. Serve on lettuce leaves. May also be stuffed in tomato shells.

Serves 4 (115 calories each)

WINE POACHED PRAWNS

1½ pounds prawns or
large shrimp
½ cup dry white wine
1½ cups chicken bouillon
¼ teaspoon dill
½ teaspoon celery salt
½ teaspoon paprika
1 cup sliced fresh
mushrooms

1 cup chopped celery
½ cup sliced green onions
2 tablespoons cornstarch
1 tablespoon lemon juice
2 tablespoons dry sherry
1 tablespoon chopped
parsley

Shell and devein prawns; turn into large skillet. Pour on
wine and bouillon. Add dill, celery salt, and paprika.
Cover and simmer about 10 minutes until prawns turn
pink. Add mushrooms and simmer 5 minutes. Add celery
and onions and simmer 5 more minutes. Blend cornstarch with lemon juice and sherry and stir into sauce.
Cook, stirring until thick and smooth. Add parsley.

Serves 6 (105 calories each)

RED SNAPPER STEAKS

2 pounds red snapper
steaks
salt
pepper
1 tablespoon melted butter
4 tablespoons chili sauce

2 tablespoons prepared
horseradish
1 tablespoon prepared
mustard
2 tablespoons grated
American cheese

Season fish on both sides with salt and pepper. Arrange
in single layer on foil-lined broiler pan. Brush with

melted butter. Broil 2 inches from heat 8–10 minutes. Combine remaining ingredients and spread over fish. Broil 2–3 minutes more until golden.

Serves 6 (185 calories each)

TROUT WITH GRAPEFRUIT SAUCE

4 whole trout, filleted
salt
¼ cup slivered almonds
2 tablespoons frozen
    grapefruit juice
    concentrate, thawed

2 tablespoons chopped
    parsley
½ cup grapefruit sections
parsley

Sprinkle trout on both sides with salt. Place on foil-lined baking sheet. Combine almonds and grapefruit juice concentrate with parsley in saucepan. Heat and pour over fish. Bake at 450° for 10 minutes. Garnish with grapefruit sections and sprigs of parsley.

Serves 4 (255 calories each)

CRUNCHY TUNA SALAD

1 envelope unflavored
  gelatin
1 10½-ounce can beef
  bouillon
2 green peppers, chopped
½ cup chopped onion
1 7-ounce can tuna fish
  (water-packed), drained
  and flaked

¾ cup coarsely chopped
  tomato
1 cup shredded lettuce
4 teaspoons lemon juice
½ teaspoon seasoned salt
¼ teaspoon seasoned
  pepper

Sprinkle gelatin over bouillon; let stand 5 minutes to soften. Bring bouillon to boil; add peppers and onion and boil only 30 seconds. Pour into bowl and set over ice. Chill until thickened, about 30 minutes. Add tuna, tomato, shredded lettuce, lemon juice, salt, and pepper to bouillon. Mix well. Pour into small loaf pan. Chill. Unmold to serve.

Serves 6 (60 calories each)

BOUILLABAISE SALAD

½ cup crabmeat
1 cup lobster meat
½ pound cooked shrimp
1 cup cooked white fish,
  flaked
2 tomatoes, sliced
1 cucumber, finely
  chopped

6 ripe olives, sliced
¼ cup plain yogurt
½ teaspoon celery seed
½ teaspoon salt
¼ teaspoon lemon pepper
¼ teaspoon garlic powder

Combine seafood with tomatoes, cucumber, and olives. Combine remaining ingredients for dressing and toss together. Serve on lettuce cups.

Serves 6 (135 calories each)

CIOPPINO

1 onion, chopped
1 green pepper, chopped
½ cup sliced celery
1 carrot, peeled and shredded
3 cloves garlic, crushed
1 tablespoon olive oil
2 16-ounce cans tomatoes
1 8-ounce can tomato sauce
1 teaspoon basil
1 bay leaf
1 teaspoon salt
¼ teaspoon pepper
1 pound halibut
1 dozen mussels or clams, in the shell
1½ cups dry white wine
½ pound shrimp, cleaned
½ pound scallops
parsley

In a dutch oven cook onion, green pepper, celery, carrot, and garlic in olive oil until soft. Stir in tomatoes, tomato sauce, basil, bay leaf, salt, and pepper. Bring to boil, then cover and simmer 2 hours. Discard bay leaf. Meanwhile cut halibut into serving pieces, scrub mussel or clam shells. Stir wine into tomato mixture. Add fish, shrimp, and scallops. Cover and simmer 10 minutes. Place mussels or clams in a layer on top of fish. Cover and steam 5-10 minutes until shells are wide open. Sprinkle with parsley. Serve in soup bowls.

Serves 8 (160 calories each)

VEGETABLES

Going the culinary route from frozen peas to frozen beans with an occasional foray into the adventure of frozen broccoli is pretty dull fare for the dieter and for the family. Branch out! Try every sort of vegetable in the frozen food department. You may not like them all, but who knows, you may hit upon a new favorite.

Then really break away from the routine and use fresh vegetables. When they are garden fresh and in season there is nothing better, and even out of season some fresh vegetables just cannot be frozen so you will add variety to the menu even if you have to pay a bit more.

Having been brought up on plain buttered vegetables,

I was doubly challenged to find new and interesting ways to serve them butterless. My spice rack proved to be the answer. I found nutmeg delicious on asparagus, caraway seeds lovely with cooked celery. Green beans go well with either marjoram or mint; peas with basil. Broccoli can be zipped up with lemon juice and tarragon; carrots are good with cinnamon and a few drops of vanilla. Try cauliflower with grated lemon rind and a sprinkle of paprika. Use your imagination and make new combinations.

Cook two vegetables together, such as peas and celery, and if you still eat your one cup's worth you will be within the limits of the diet plan. Instead of cooking vegetables in plain salted water, add a few granules of powdered chicken stock base to the water. And never overcook your vegetables. You'll cook away their vitamins as well as their flavor.

Some of the recipes in the main dish section of this book will call for vegetables cooked with the meat, poultry, or seafood. When that happens you must not prepare another cooked vegetable for that meal but merely add raw vegetables or salad to the menu.

One final word: if you find room for 13 extra calories one day treat yourself to a tablespoonful of Yogurt Hollandaise (page 124) on your asparagus or broccoli. It's really divine.

HERBED ARTICHOKES

2 10-ounce packages
  frozen artichoke hearts
½ cup water
1 tablespoon olive oil
2 tablespoons white wine
1 tablespoon lemon juice
½ teaspoon salt

4 peppercorns
1 bay leaf
1 clove garlic, crushed
¼ teaspoon thyme
¼ teaspoon tarragon
sprig of parsley

Combine all ingredients and simmer for 5 minutes until artichoke hearts are tender. Remove artichokes to bowl. Cook liquid down, uncovered, for 10 minutes more. Strain liquid over artichokes. Chill for several hours or overnight. Serve cold.

Serves 8 (35 calories each)

ASPARAGUS VINAIGRETTE

1 7-ounce jar pimientos
1 16-ounce jar asparagus
  spears, drained
¾ cup tomato juice
¼ cup vinegar
1 teaspoon salt
¼ teaspoon pepper
1 teaspoon sugar

⅛ teaspoon paprika
1 teaspoon chopped onion
3 tablespoons chopped
  dill pickle
1 tablespoon chopped
  parsley
4 lettuce leaves

Cut pimiento into 1-inch strips and wrap strips around each asparagus spear in spiral fashion. Place in shallow container. Combine remaining ingredients, except lettuce, and blend until smooth. Pour over asparagus and marinate at least one hour. Remove from marinade and serve on lettuce leaves.

Serves 4 (40 calories each)

GREEN BEANS MANHATTAN

3 cups cut green beans
2 4-ounce cans sliced mushrooms
½ cup dry white wine
1½ teaspoons chicken stock base

1½ tablespoons cornstarch
½ teaspoon salt
1 tablespoon minced chives

Cook beans in boiling salted water just until tender, about 10 minutes. Meanwhile drain mushroom liquid into measuring cup. Combine half cup mushroom liquid with wine, chicken stock base, cornstarch, salt, and chives in a small saucepan. Cook, stirring, until mixture boils and thickens. Stir in mushrooms. Drain beans well and combine with sauce.

Serves 8 (25 calories each)

SAVORY STRING BEANS

1 onion, chopped
1 clove garlic, crushed
1 teaspoon oil
1 teaspoon minced savory
1 tomato, peeled and diced
1 tablespoon minced green pepper
1 tablespoon minced celery
1 tablespoon chopped parsley
1 tablespoon dry white wine
salt
pepper
1 pound string beans, cooked

Sauté onion and garlic in oil until lightly browned. Add all remaining ingredients except beans. Simmer for 10 minutes. Pour sauce over cooked beans and mix well.

Serves 6 (40 calories each)

PICKLED BEETS

1 16-ounce can sliced beets
1 onion, thinly sliced
1 clove garlic, halved
1/3 cup red wine
1/3 cup red wine vinegar
2 tablespoons sugar
1/4 teaspoon salt
6 peppercorns
4 whole cloves
1 bay leaf
1 teaspoon celery seed

Drain beets, reserving 3/4 cup liquid. Arrange beets alternately with onion slices in quart jar; add garlic. In saucepan combine reserved beet liquid with remaining ingredients, bring to boil. Pour over contents in jar. Let stand uncovered at room temperature until cool; then cover and chill at least 24 hours before serving. Shake jar every once in a while to distribute seasonings. Remove garlic after several hours.

Serves 6 (65 calories each)

HERBED BROCCOLI

1 bunch broccoli
1 cup salted water
4 tablespoons lemon juice
1 clove garlic, crushed

¼ teaspoon oregano
¼ teaspoon salt
freshly ground black
pepper

Trim broccoli, simmer for 20 minutes in salted water until tender. Combine and heat remaining ingredients and pour over broccoli.

Serves 6 (22 calories each)

HUNGARIAN BRUSSELS SPROUTS

8 ounces canned tomatoes,
drained
1 green pepper, chopped
1 bay leaf
1 teaspoon caraway seeds

½ teaspoon paprika
salt and pepper to taste
8 ounces brussels
sprouts, cooked and
drained

Combine all ingredients except brussels sprouts and simmer 8–10 minutes, until green pepper is tender. Cut cooked sprouts in half and combine with tomato mixture. Heat thoroughly.

Serves 4 (30 calories each)

HOT SLAW, DANISH STYLE

8 cups shredded cabbage
1 teaspoon salt
1 teaspoon dry mustard
2 teaspoons sugar
¼ teaspoon pepper
2 tablespoons flour

1 egg
1 tablespoon butter
¾ cup skimmed milk
¼ cup cider vinegar
chopped parsley

Cook cabbage in enough salted boiling water to cover it until tender-crisp, about 5 minutes. Drain well and keep warm. Combine and beat together salt, mustard, sugar, pepper, flour, and egg. Melt butter in top of double boiler. Stir in egg mixture and milk. Slowly add vinegar, beating constantly, until sauce is thick and smooth. Fold in cabbage and mix well. Sprinkle with parsley.

Serves 8 (55 calories each)

PEASANT CABBAGE

1-pound head green cabbage
¼ cup water
½ teaspoon caraway seeds
1 chicken bouillon cube

1 green apple, peeled and cubed
1 onion, chopped
2 tablespoons cider vinegar
2 teaspoons Worcester-shire sauce

Shred cabbage, add water. Cover and cook over low heat 10 minutes. Add remaining ingredients. Cover and cook 15 minutes more.

Serves 6 (40 calories each)

THREE-MINUTE CABBAGE

¾ cup skimmed milk
½ teaspoon salt
dash nutmeg
2 teaspoons butter

3 cups shredded cabbage
2 teaspoons cornstarch
2 tablespoons dry sherry

Heat milk, salt, nutmeg, and butter to boiling. Add cabbage and boil 2 minutes, stirring frequently. Blend cornstarch with sherry; stir into cabbage. Boil 1 minute more, stirring constantly.

Serves 4 (55 calories each)

CARROTS IN DILLED WINE

1 tablespoon butter
½ teaspoon dried dill weed
½ cup dry white wine
2 teaspoons minced onion
½ cup chicken bouillon

2 teaspoons cornstarch
¼ teaspoon garlic salt
2 drops hot pepper sauce
3 cups hot, cooked sliced carrots

Melt butter in saucepan; add dill, wine, and onion. Combine bouillon with cornstarch. Add to contents of pan along with garlic salt and hot pepper sauce. Cook, stirring, over moderate heat until sauce thickens. Add carrots, lower heat, and simmer 5 minutes.

Serves 6 (45 calories each)

GINGER CARROTS

2 cups sliced carrots   grated rind of 1 orange
½ teaspoon ginger

Cook carrots in boiling salted water 5–8 minutes. Drain well, then sprinkle with ginger and grated orange rind.

Serves 4 (25 calories each)

CAULIFLOWER ORIENTALE

1 whole cauliflower   1 tablespoon soy sauce
½ cup chicken bouillon   1 tablespoon grated lemon
                                             rind

Simmer cauliflower in chicken bouillon until tender, about 20 minutes. Drain and sprinkle with soy sauce and lemon rind.

Serves 6 (20 calories each)

CAULIFLOWER PANCAKES

1 cup cold, cooked   1 teaspoon grated onion
     cauliflower   ½ teaspoon salt
1 egg   ½ teaspoon lemon pepper
2 tablespoons grated   1 teaspoon butter
     Parmesan cheese

Mash cauliflower and combine with egg, cheese, onion, and seasoning. Melt butter in 7-inch teflon frying pan.

Put cauliflower mixture into pan and sauté for 5 minutes until brown on bottom. Cut into quarters and turn over. Brown for 3 minutes on second side.

Serves 4 (45 calories each)

POLKA DOT CAULI-FLOWERS

1 head cauliflower, broken into florets
½ cup water
1 tablespoon chicken stock base
1 clove garlic, crushed

1 tablespoon chopped parsley
2 teaspoons lemon juice
pepper to taste
3 tablespoons roasted peppers, diced

Cook cauliflower until just slightly underdone. Combine remaining ingredients; bring them to a boil, then pour over cauliflower.

Serves 4 (20 calories each)

TARRAGON CELERY

3 celery hearts
1 cup chicken bouillon
¼ cup sherry

1 teaspoon tarragon
¼ teaspoon salt

Wash celery and cut into 1-inch pieces. Place in saucepan with remaining ingredients. Simmer until tender, about 15 minutes. Drain, sprinkle with paprika, and serve warm or chilled.

Serves 4 (18 calories each)

PICKLED CUKES

2 medium cucumbers	2 teaspoons minced fresh
2 teaspoons salt	ginger root (from a
½ cup white vinegar	Chinese store)
⅓ cup sugar	2 teaspoons sesame seeds

Wash cucumbers and pare lengthwise in ¼–½-inch strips, leaving every other strip of green skin on. Cut in halves, lengthwise; remove seeds and slice thinly. Put in bowl and add salt. Mix well and let stand 1 hour. Put in cloth and squeeze out excess moisture. Mix remaining ingredients and bring to a boil. Pour over cucumbers and chill several hours. Drain before serving.

Serves 4 (80 calories each)

EGGPLANT ORIENTALE

4 small eggplants	1 clove garlic, crushed
½ cup sliced mushrooms	1 teaspoon salt
½ cup chopped onion	¼ teaspoon pepper
3 tablespoons flour	1 teaspoon chopped mint
½ pint plain yogurt	

Split eggplant lengthwise, cook in salted water until tender, 10–15 minutes. Scoop out and dice pulp, leaving ¼-inch shell. Combine eggplant pulp, mushrooms, and onion, and cook together for 5 minutes. Sprinkle with flour; cook 2 minutes. Add yogurt and stir until thick and smooth. Add seasonings. Fill shells. Bake at 350° for 20–30 minutes.

Serves 8 (50 calories each)

EGGPLANT PROVENÇALE

1 tablespoon olive oil
1 eggplant, peeled and
 diced
2 cloves garlic, crushed
1 green pepper, diced
3 tomatoes, skinned and
 diced

½ pound mushrooms,
 sliced
1 teaspoon salt
1 teaspoon basil
1 tablespoon chopped
 parsley

Heat oil in skillet and sauté eggplant and garlic until
lightly browned. Add remaining ingredients and simmer,
uncovered, 10 minutes, until eggplant is tender.

Serves 6 (50 calories each)

BAKED STUFFED MUSHROOMS

1 10-ounce package frozen
 chopped spinach
16 medium mushrooms
1 tablespoon chopped
 onion
1 teaspoon Worcester-
 shire sauce

dash hot pepper sauce
¼ teaspoon thyme
salt and pepper to taste
1 teaspoon chopped
 chives

Cook spinach and drain. Wash mushrooms, remove
stems and chop them fine. Reserve caps. Combine
spinach, chopped stems, and remaining ingredients.
Spoon into caps and place in shallow pan. Bake at 375°
for 20 minutes.

Serves 4 (25 calories each)

CHINESE SPINACH

1 10-ounce package frozen chopped spinach
1 cup bean sprouts
1 4-ounce can sliced mushrooms
½ onion, minced
salt and pepper to taste
½ clove garlic, crushed

Cook spinach and drain. Toss together with remaining ingredients and heat through.

Serves 4 (25 calories each)

CREAMED SPINACH

2 10-ounce packages frozen chopped spinach
2 cups boiled onions, drained
⅓ cup instant non-fat dry milk powder
1 teaspoon salt
dash nutmeg
dash white pepper
1 teaspoon chicken stock base

Cook spinach and drain. Combine remaining ingredients in blender until smooth. Add spinach to mixture in 1-quart casserole and bake at 350° for 20 minutes.

Serves 6 (50 calories each)

SPINACH AND CHEESE CASSEROLE

2 10-ounce packages frozen chopped spinach
1 cup low-fat cottage cheese
2 eggs, beaten
1 teaspoon minced onion
1/4 teaspoon nutmeg
1 teaspoon seasoned salt
1/4 teaspoon seasoned pepper
2 tablespoons grated Parmesan cheese

Cook spinach, then drain well. Add all remaining ingredients except Parmesan cheese. Place in 9-inch pie plate and sprinkle with grated cheese. Bake at 350° for 25 minutes.

Serves 8 (50 calories each)

GOURMET SPINACH

2 10-ounce packages frozen chopped spinach
2 4-ounce cans mushrooms, stems and pieces
1 tablespoon minced onion
2 cloves garlic, crushed
1 teaspoon salt
1 tablespoon powdered chicken stock base
pepper to taste
1/2 cup plain yogurt

Cook spinach and drain thoroughly. Drain canned mushrooms. Combine and heat together all ingredients except yogurt. Then stir in yogurt and reheat briefly.

Serves 6 (30 calories each)

SPINACH PUDDING

2 10-ounce packages frozen
   chopped spinach, cooked
   and drained
2 cups low-fat cottage
   cheese

1 teaspoon salt
2 tablespoons grated
   Parmesan cheese
2 eggs

Mix together all ingredients and pour into 1-quart casserole. Bake at 350° for 30 minutes.

Serves 8 (75 calories each)

SPINACH SOUFFLÉ

1 10-ounce package frozen
   chopped spinach
1 cup plain yogurt

1 egg, separated
1 teaspoon sugar
dash onion salt

Cook spinach and drain thoroughly. Combine with yogurt, egg yolk, sugar, and salt. Beat egg white stiff, then fold in. Bake at 350° for 15 minutes.

Serves 4 (65 calories each)

SQUASH MEDLEY

1 10-ounce package frozen
   zucchini
1 10-ounce package frozen
   crookneck squash
1 tablespoon chicken
   stock base

1 7-ounce jar pimientos,
   cut in strips
1/4 teaspoon garlic powder
1/2 teaspoon dry onion
   flakes
1/2 teaspoon salt
dash pepper

Cook squash, drain well, and add remaining ingredients. Heat through and serve hot.

Serves 4 (30 calories each)

SQUASH PANCAKES

1 12-ounce package frozen cooked squash	1 teaspoon onion salt
1 egg	1 tablespoon flour
	1 teaspoon baking powder

Defrost squash and drain well. Combine with egg, salt, flour, and baking powder. Drop by heaping tablespoons onto heated teflon frying pan and heat until brown; turn to brown second side.

Serves 8 (65 calories each)

SQUASH TOMATO SCALLOP

⅓ cup finely chopped green onions	2 cups coarsely chopped tomatoes
1 teaspoon butter	¼ cup dry white wine
2 cups thinly sliced summer squash	2 teaspoons chicken stock base

Cook onion in butter until soft but not browned. Stir in squash and tomatoes. Add remaining ingredients. Simmer about 15 minutes, until squash is just tender.

Serves 4 (45 calories each)

ROSEY TOMATOES

2 pounds fresh tomatoes
1/4 cup chopped onion
1/2 teaspoon dried dill
    weed

1 teaspoon celery seed
1 teaspoon salt
1/2 teaspoon pepper
1/2 cup clam-tomato juice

Combine all ingredients and simmer 15 minutes.

Serves 8 (30 calories each)

STUFFED TOMATOES

4 tomatoes
1 green pepper, minced
1/2 onion, minced

1 teaspoon salt
1 clove garlic, crushed

Scoop insides from tomatoes. Mix tomato pulp with remaining ingredients and stuff back into tomato shells. Bake at 350° for 10–15 minutes.

Serves 4 (30 calories each)

WESTERN ZUCCHINI

3/4 cup chopped onion
1 tablespoon cooking oil
1/2 cup chopped celery
1/2 cup chopped green
    pepper
1 16-ounce can tomatoes
1/2 clove garlic, crushed

1 teaspoon salt
1/2 teaspoon pepper
2 pound zucchini, cubed
2 tablespoons chopped
    parsley
1 tablespoon grated
    Parmesan cheese

Sauté onion in oil until transparent. Add celery, green pepper, tomatoes, and garlic. Season with salt and pepper. Simmer for 30 minutes. Add large cubes of zucchini and simmer until tender, about 30 minutes more. Sprinkle with parsley and grated Parmesan cheese.

Serves 8 (50 calories each)

CHINESE VEGETABLES

½ cup dried mushrooms
1 cup celery, sliced

1 7-ounce package frozen
   pea pods
1 teaspoon soy sauce

Pour warm water over mushrooms to cover and let sit for 20 minutes to soften. Drain and slice. Cook celery in salted water for 5 minutes. Cook pea pods as directed on package. Toss all vegetables together with soy sauce to serve.

Serves 6 (25 calories each)

ITALIAN VEGETABLE CASSEROLE

1 tablespoon olive oil
1 onion, cut in rings
1 green pepper, cut in strips
1 small eggplant, diced
1 4-ounce can sliced mushrooms
1 16-ounce can tomatoes

1 teaspoon salt
1/4 teaspoon pepper
1/2 teaspoon basil
1 teaspoon oregano
1 tablespoon Worcestershire sauce
2 tablespoons grated Parmesan cheese

In large skillet sauté onion and green pepper in oil until soft. Add eggplant and mushrooms and sauté all together. Add remaining ingredients. Mix thoroughly and place in casserole; bake at 350° for 30 minutes.

Serves 6 (65 calories each)

ORIENTAL VEGETABLES

1 tablespoon vegetable oil
1 cup diagonally sliced carrots
1 cup sliced cauliflower
1/2 cup sliced celery
1/2 cup sliced green pepper
1/4 cup diced onion

3/4 cup water
1 can bamboo shoots
1 cup fresh pineapple chunks
2 tablespoons soy sauce
1/2 teaspoon salt
2 teaspoons cornstarch

Sauté all vegetables in oil until coated and shiny. Add water; cover and simmer for 10 minutes. Add bamboo shoots and pineapple. Mix together remaining ingredients and stir into vegetables. Cook and stir until sauce begins to thicken, about 2–3 minutes.

Serves 8 (45 calories each)

RATATOUILLE

1 medium eggplant, peeled and diced
1 tablespoon olive oil
2 large onions, chopped
2 green peppers, diced
2 cloves garlic, crushed
2 zucchini, diced

1 16-ounce can tomatoes
salt and pepper to taste
2 tablespoons chopped parsley
1/8 teaspoon marjoram
1/8 teaspoon basil

Sauté eggplant in oil; add and sauté onion, peppers, and garlic. When vegetables begin to soften add zucchini and tomatoes. Add remaining ingredients. Cover and simmer 25 minutes; remove cover and simmer 10 minutes more.

Serves 6 (60 calories each)

VEGETABLE MEDLEY

1 head cauliflower, broken into florets
1 16-ounce bag frozen whole baby carrots

1 cup chopped green pepper
1 cup water
1 teaspoon salt

Combine all ingredients; bring to boil. Simmer, covered, until all vegetables are tender, about 15 minutes. Drain and serve.

Serves 12 (20 calories each)

SALADS AND DRESSINGS

Raw vegetables, as I said in the Introduction, are not only filling; they are free, calorie-wise. They are great between-meal snacks and provide the salad course at lunch and dinner. However, if you are not imaginative in varying the possibilities and combinations thereof you may suddenly begin to feel like Peter Rabbit let loose in Farmer Jones's vegetable patch. Your nose may even begin to twitch and your ears grow longer.

Truthfully, too much of the same carrots and celery sticks will be very dull, and boredom leads to cheating, God forbid! So try to vary your snacks. Keep zucchini sticks, cucumber, and green pepper chunks in a bowl of ice water in the refrigerator so it's easy to get at when the mid-afternoon hunger pangs begin.

Don't always use the same dull old iceberg lettuce in your salads. There are many more interesting varieties of lettuce such as Boston, Salad Bowl, or Romaine. And don't overlook raw spinach leaves as salad greens either.

Salad dressings are difficult for the dieter who demands quality. I've tried dozens of recipes to come up with these few and must confess nothing tastes quite so good as plain old French dressing or oil and vinegar. But oil is the problem. One tablespoon, whether olive, salad oil, peanut oil, or what have you, still counts as 125 calories. The diet dressings commercially available still contain oil but are watered down. The only oil that has absolutely no calories is mineral oil but that is also a laxative and must be used with extreme caution.

Cottage cheese substitutes protein-wise for meat at lunchtime. A lovely luncheon salad can be made by scooping out a fresh tomato and filling it with low-fat cottage cheese sprinkled with dill. Or combine cottage cheese and dill with grated radishes. Season with salt, pepper, and caraway seeds. Remember, a half cup of low-fat cottage cheese has only 75 calories; the raw vegetables, herbs, and spices are free.

ANDY'S CHINESE SALAD

This salad can be made into a full meal by adding some shredded chicken meat from one breast or some cooked shrimp.

1 16-ounce can bean sprouts or ½ pound fresh bean sprouts	¼ teaspoon salt
	½ teaspoon sugar
2 tablespoons soy sauce	½ sweet roasted pepper, diced
2 tablespoons wine vinegar	½ fresh green pepper, slivered
1 teaspoon peanut oil	6 black olives, diced
1 teaspoon sesame seed oil	5 water chestnuts, diced

If canned bean sprouts are used, drain and soak sprouts in cold water overnight. Drain before use. If fresh bean sprouts are used, wash, then pour plenty of boiling water over the sprouts to cook them slightly without actually boiling. Let sit 5 minutes, then drain, cool with cold water, and drain again. Fresh bean sprouts are preferred to canned ones where available.

Mix soy sauce, vinegar, both oils, salt, and sugar in bowl. Add the suggested vegetables or any others you choose to the bean sprouts, then pour dressing over mixture and stir thoroughly. Serve cold.

Serves 6 (35 calories each)

ANTIPASTO SALAD

1 10-ounce package
frozen French style
green beans
1 4-ounce can sliced
mushrooms

1 4-ounce jar roasted red
peppers
½ cup red wine vinegar
½ teaspoon oregano
salt and pepper to taste
1 clove garlic, crushed

Cook beans, drain, and cool. Add drained mushrooms, peppers. Pour vinegar over all. Add seasonings, mix thoroughly. Chill.

Serves 4 (20 calories each)

APPLE ENDIVE SALAD

3 eating apples, preferably
red
½ pound Belgian endive,
sliced ¼ inch thick

½ 6-ounce can frozen
orange juice concen-
trate, thawed
6 filberts, chopped

Core apples and cut in thin wedges. Arrange in alternate layers with endive in glass bowl. Pour orange juice concentrate on top and sprinkle with nuts.

Serves 6 (75 calories each)

BEAN SALAD

1 9-ounce package frozen cut green beans
1 9-ounce package frozen cut wax beans
2 tablespoons diced pimiento
½ teaspoon grated lemon rind
½ teaspoon salt
1 tablespoon sugar
1 tablespoon oil
1 tablespoon cider vinegar

Cook beans together in 1 cup salted water for 10 minutes. Drain. Add remaining ingredients and toss well. Chill for several hours before serving.

Serves 8 (30 calories each)

BEET SALAD

1 16-ounce can diced beets
½ cup beet liquid
¼ cup vinegar
¼ teaspoon pepper
½ teaspoon salt
1 teaspoon chopped fresh dill
2 cucumbers, sliced

Place all ingredients except cucumbers in a jar and chill thoroughly. At serving time add cucumbers. Serve on lettuce cups.

Serves 8 (25 calories each)

CELERY VICTOR

2 cups celery, cut into
2-inch pieces

½ cup beef bouillon
½ cup dry white wine

Cook celery in wine and bouillon about 20 minutes. Allow celery to cool in wine broth, then drain and serve as salad.

Serves 4 (16 calories each)

CHABLIS ASPIC SALAD

2 envelopes unflavored
gelatin
3¼ cups tomato juice
¾ cup Chablis wine

2 tablespoons prepared
horseradish
2 tablespoons lemon juice
1 teaspoon salt

Soften gelatin in ½ cup tomato juice. Heat remaining tomato juice and dissolve gelatin in it. Blend in remaining ingredients and pour into 5-cup ring mold. Chill until firm. Unmold on bed of salad greens. Center may be filled with cottage cheese, fish salad, or marinated cooked vegetables, but you must count the calories for the filling.

Serves 8 (50 calories each)

CHINESE CUCUMBER SALAD

2 medium cucumbers
½ teaspoon salt
1 teaspoon soy sauce
1 tablespoon sugar

1 tablespoon vinegar
2 teaspoons sesame seed
   oil (from a Chinese
   store)

Peel cucumbers and cut in half lengthwise. Remove seeds. Cut into ¼-inch slices. Mix remaining ingredients and pour over cucumbers just before serving. Toss well.

Serves 4 (28 calories each)

CITRUS CIRCLE SALAD

2 medium red onions
2 grapefruit, sectioned
2 oranges, sectioned
4 cups torn spinach leaves

2 cups torn salad greens
4 tablespoons Horseradish
   Dressing (See page 122)

* See page 178.

Slice onion thinly and separate into rings. Arrange fruit and onion on mixed greens and toss with Horseradish Dressing.

Serves 8 (70 calories each)

CREAMY CUKES

½ cup plain yogurt
grated juice and rind of
half lemon
½ teaspoon salt

1 tablespoon dill weed
1 teaspoon sugar
2 cucumbers, sliced paper
thin

Blend yogurt, juice, rind, and seasoning. Toss with cucumbers, chill several hours. Great with fish!

Serves 4 (35 calories each)

CUCUMBER SALAD

3 cups sliced cucumbers
1 medium green pepper,
seeded and cut into
rings
½ cup sliced green onions
2 tablespoons vegetable
oil

2 tablespoons lemon
juice
2 tablespoons vinegar
1 teaspoon sugar
¼ teaspoon dill weed
8 lettuce cups

In large bowl combine cucumbers, green pepper, and green onions. Blend together oil, lemon juice, vinegar, sugar, and dill. Pour over vegetables; toss lightly. Cover and refrigerate 1 hour. Toss several times. Serve in lettuce cups.

Serves 8 (35 calories each)

FILLED TOMATO RINGS

1 envelope unflavored
gelatin
2 cups clam-tomato juice
½ teaspoon salt
¼ teaspoon celery salt
1 bay leaf
dash pepper
dash ground cloves
1 cup low-fat cottage
cheese

¼ cup finely chopped,
unpeeled cucumber
2 tablespoons chopped
green pepper
1 tablespoon chopped
pimiento
1 teaspoon grated onion
¼ teaspoon salt

Soften gelatin in ½ cup clam-tomato juice. In a 2-quart saucepan combine rest of juice, salt, celery salt, bay leaf, pepper, and cloves. Heat to boiling; simmer 5 minutes. Add softened gelatin and stir to dissolve. Remove bay leaf. Pour into 6 individual ½-cup ring molds. Chill until firm. To prepare filling, combine cottage cheese with remaining ingredients. Chill. Unmold rings onto salad greens; fill centers with cottage cheese mixture.

Serves 6 (40 calories each)

GREEN AND WHITE SALAD

½ medium-size cauliflower
½ pound fresh spinach
2 tablespoons salad oil
1 tablespoon white wine
vinegar
1 clove garlic, crushed

½ teaspoon salt
½ teaspoon dry mustard
½ teaspoon basil
¼ teaspoon pepper
dash nutmeg

Rinse and drain cauliflower and coarsely chop. Wash spinach, pat dry, remove tough stems. Slice leaves into 1/4-inch strips. Combine cauliflower and spinach. In small jar combine oil, vinegar, garlic, salt, mustard, basil, pepper, and nutmeg. Blend well. When ready to serve, toss salad with dressing.

Serves 6 (60 calories each)

GREEN BEAN AND SPROUT SALAD

1 10-ounce package frozen French style green beans
1 cup bean sprouts
1/4 cup minced green onions

1 pimiento, minced
1 tablespoon vegetable oil
1 tablespoon cider vinegar
salt and lemon pepper
1/2 teaspoon sugar

Cook beans until tender-crisp; drain and cool. Add bean sprouts, green onions, and pimiento. Toss to mix. Combine oil, vinegar, and seasonings; pour over vegetables. Toss and chill.

Serves 4 (55 calories each)

HUNGARIAN CUCUMBER SALAD

1 cup plain yogurt
1 teaspoon coarse salt
1/2 teaspoon paprika
2 medium cucumbers, peeled and sliced

2 medium tomatoes, quartered
1 onion, sliced in rings
1 green pepper, diced

Blend yogurt with salt and paprika. Mix well with combined vegetables. Chill before serving.

Serves 6 (45 calories each)

SILLSALAD

1 8-ounce jar herring tidbits in wine sauce

1 16-ounce can diced beets, drained

2 cups diced apple

2 tablespoons honey

4 tablespoons lemon juice

Drain sauce from herring. Chop herring, beets, and apple coarsely. Add honey and lemon juice; blend well. Chill thoroughly. Serve in lettuce cups.

Serves 8 (100 calories each)

VEGETABLE JUICE ASPIC

2 envelopes unflavored gelatin

2 12-ounce cans vegetable juice cocktail

1 9-ounce can artichoke hearts, drained and halved

1 tablespoon prepared horseradish

1 tablespoon Worcestershire sauce

2 tablespoons minced chives

In small saucepan sprinkle gelatin over 1 cup vegetable juice to soften. Heat and stir until gelatin is dissolved. Remove from heat and add remaining juice and other

ingredients. Pour into 2-quart mold and chill until firm.
Unmold and serve on salad greens.

Serves 8 (35 calories each)

VEGETABLE SALAD

2 tomatoes, sliced
½ cup cooked green beans
1 cucumber, sliced
1 zucchini, sliced
½ cup sliced raw
  mushrooms
2 carrots, cut into thin
  strips

½ cup sliced radishes
1 Bermuda onion, sliced
  in rings
1 cup raw cauliflower
  florets
mixed greens
4 tablespoons Low Cal
  Herb Dressing (See
  page 122)

Marinate vegetables in Low Cal Herb Dressing at least
4 hours in refrigerator. When ready to serve, toss with
greens.

Serves 8 (35 calories each)

ZERO SALAD

ZERO DRESSING

½ cup tomato juice
2 tablespoons lemon juice
  or vinegar

1 tablespoon onion, finely
  chopped
salt and pepper to taste

MIXED VEGETABLE SALAD

Lettuce, cucumber, celery, green pepper
Chicory, tomato, radish
Lettuce, parsley, raw cauliflower, tomato
Escarole, tomato, cucumber
Cabbage, celery, green pepper
Lettuce, watercress, cucumber
Lettuce, raw spinach, radish

Any combination of raw vegetables combined with Zero Dressing may be eaten in unlimited amount with virtually no calorie count.

ZUCCHINI SALAD

1½ pounds zucchini
1 small onion, diced
2 tablespoons chopped fresh dill
1 tablespoon chopped parsley
1 teaspoon salt
1 teaspoon oregano
1 tablespoon lemon juice
1 teaspoon honey
1 cup plain yogurt

Scrub zucchini and slice paper thin. Combine with all remaining ingredients and refrigerate at least 1 hour before serving.

Serves 6 (50 calories each)

COTTAGE DILL DRESSING

1 cup low-fat cottage
  cheese
1 tablespoon lemon juice
1 teaspoon dill weed
½ teaspoon celery seed

½ teaspoon sugar
⅛ teaspoon grated lemon
  rind
3 tablespoons skim milk

Combine all ingredients and blend until smooth. Cover and chill.

Makes 1½ cups (7 calories per tablespoon)

FLORIDA SALAD DRESSING

2 teaspoons cornstarch
1 teaspoon sugar
¾ teaspoon salt
⅛ teaspoon pepper
½ teaspoon paprika

½ teaspoon dry mustard
1 cup grapefruit juice
2 tablespoons salad oil
¼ cup catsup

Combine dry ingredients in saucepan; stir in grapefruit juice. Place over medium heat and bring to boil, stirring constantly. Boil for 1 minute. Remove from heat; stir in remaining ingredients. Chill.

Makes 1¼ cups (22 calories per tablespoon)

HORSERADISH DRESSING

8 ounces plain yogurt
1 tablespoon white
  prepared horseradish
1 tablespoon tarragon
  vinegar
1 tablespoon chopped dill

1 tablespoon chopped
  chives
1 tablespoon sugar
¾ teaspoon salt
¼ teaspoon paprika

Combine all ingredients. Cover and chill at least 4 hours.

Makes 1 cup (10 calories per tablespoon)

LOW CAL HERB DRESSING

½ cup frozen grapefruit
  juice concentrate,
  thawed
½ cup water
⅓ cup wine vinegar
½ clove garlic, crushed
1 tablespoon paprika

1 teaspoon sugar
1 teaspoon salt
½ teaspoon ground ginger
¼ teaspoon marjoram
¼ teaspoon hot pepper
  sauce
1 tablespoon oil

Combine all ingredients in jar or bowl. Shake or beat well. Let stand at least 1 hour before serving.

Makes 1 cup (22 calories per tablespoon)

RUSSIAN DRESSING

1½ cups garden salad
   cottage cheese
1 tablespoon lemon juice
½ teaspoon salt
¼ teaspoon pepper

1 clove garlic, crushed
1 teaspoon basil
1 teaspoon dill weed
½ cup clam-tomato juice
1 hard-cooked egg

Combine all ingredients except egg in blender and whirl until smooth. Just before serving, chop egg fine and stir into dressing.

Makes 2 cups (15 calories per tablespoon)

SLIM JIM SALAD DRESSING

1 tablespoon cornstarch
1 tablespoon sugar
1 teaspoon dry mustard
¾ teaspoon salt
⅛ teaspoon pepper

2 egg yolks, lightly beaten
¾ cup dry white wine
2 tablespoons white wine
   vinegar
1 tablespoon salad oil

Blend cornstarch, sugar, mustard, salt, and pepper together in a small saucepan. Add egg yolks, wine, and vinegar; mix until smooth. Cook and stir over medium heat until mixture is smooth and thickened and barely reaches a boil. Remove from heat and blend in oil. Cover and chill before using. If dressing separates stir gently before using.

Makes 1 cup (20 calories per tablespoon)

V-8 SALAD DRESSING

1 12-ounce can vegetable
  juice cocktail (V-8)
2 tablespoons vinegar
1 teaspoon prepared
  mustard

dash paprika
1 teaspoon Worcester-
  shire sauce

Combine all ingredients in jar; shake until blended.
Makes 1½ cups (3 calories per tablespoon)

YOGURT HOLLANDAISE

2 egg yolks
¾ cup plain yogurt

½ tablespoon lemon juice
dash paprika

Beat egg yolks; add yogurt and lemon juice. Stir in top
of double boiler over hot water until thickened and
smooth. Add paprika. Serve with asparagus or broccoli.
Makes 1 cup (13 calories per tablespoon)

YOGURT RUSSIAN DRESSING

½ pint plain yogurt

½ cup chili sauce

Blend well.
Makes 1½ cups (10 calories per tablespoon)

DESSERTS

Desserts in a diet cookbook? What, never? No, never! Never? Well, hardly ever. My original concept was that there would be no desserts at all, but I have found myself craving a sweet finish to a meal and know this must be an almost universal feeling.

As I told you in the introduction, two fruits a day should be included in the diet in addition to a citrus, such as orange juice, for breakfast. I also noted that this fruit sugar provides instant gratification for a craving for sweets. It is not necessary to eat your dessert fruit at the end of the meal, though you may if you wish. The fruit may certainly be saved for a between- or after-meal snack.

Most of my dessert recipes are for fruit combinations. A few others appear, but you will note they are all under 100 calories per serving. Also, please be aware of the calorie count of various raw fruits because they are not all the same. An apple has 100 calories, as does a pear, a banana, 4/5 cup of cherries, 20–25 grapes, 1/3 of a honeydew melon, a nectarine, an orange, or (surprise of all surprises) a slice of watermelon. Less caloric fruits in the 50-calorie range are 1/2 cup blueberries, a half cantaloupe or grapefruit, a peach, and a cup of raspberries or strawberries. In the 25-calorie range fall a tangerine or plum. Canned fruits packed in medium or heavy syrup have many more calories than raw. And dried fruits are staggering: 4 dried apricots or 2 dates are 50 calories; 3 small figs, 150; 4 prunes, 150; and 1/3 cup seedless raisins, 160!

The Calorie Countdown in the back of the book (page 137) does not mention the no-nos, but if you do plan to cheat you should have some idea of what you are in for. One plain chocolate bar is 250 calories; a piece of chocolate cake, 150; fruit cake, 300; a brownie, 200. A half cup of chocolate ice cream is 250, but vanilla is only 200. A half cup of sherbet is 200 calories too, as is a doughnut. A slice of pie, such as apple, berry, or lemon meringue, is 350, and an ice cream sundae is 400.

I have a personal theory about eating cake, pie, or cookies. If it's homemade and delicious I find it hard to resist, but I can try to be sensible about a piece of pastry that's been put together from a mix or bought in a bakery. If I'm going to consume forbidden calories at least I make sure I get my calories' worth. Always ask yourself if the temptation in front of you is really worth the calories that will be consumed. Often when your conscience becomes your guide it's easier to say "no, thank you" than to live the rest of the day with guilt feelings.

CANTALOUPE AND PINEAPPLE BASKETS

1 small fresh pineapple
2 cantaloupes

1 tablespoon chopped mint leaves

Cut pineapple in half lengthwise; scoop out fruit and dice it, discarding core. Cut cantaloupes in half, remove seeds, and make fruit into balls. Combine fruit with mint and spoon into shells for pretty presentation. Serve well chilled.

Serves 6 (65 calories each)

CANTALOUPE RASPBERRY REFRESHER

2 cups raspberries

1 large cantaloupe

Wash and drain berries; force through wire strainer to make ½ cup puree. Cut melon into bite-size chunks, cutting off rind and discarding seeds. Mix cantaloupe and raspberry puree. Serve in sherbet glasses.

Serves 8 (33 calories each)

CANTALOUPE WITH STRAWBERRY SAUCE

1 cup strawberries
1 tablespoon sugar

2 tablespoons lemon juice
2 cantaloupes, halved and
   seeded

Mash strawberries and combine with sugar and lemon juice (may be done in blender). Pour sauce into cantaloupe halves and chill at least one hour.

Serves 4 (85 calories each)

CONFETTI COMPOTE

1 pint lime sherbet
1 pint fresh strawberries

1 cantaloupe

Dip melon baller in warm water and scoop sherbet into small balls. Place on chilled cookie sheet. Cover and store in freezer until ready to serve. Wash, stem, and chill strawberries. Scoop balls from cantaloupe. Divide melon balls, strawberries, and sherbet balls among 8 dessert dishes.

Serves 8 (80 calories each)

FLORIDA LOW-CALORIE DESSERTS

To prepare Florida grapefruit halves, cut fruit in half, remove core. Cut around each section, loosening fruit from membrane. Each grapefruit half contains 55 calories and prepared with the following toppings has less than 100 calories per serving.

	Calories
3 fresh strawberries	73
1 tablespoon raisins	78
2 teaspoons apple jelly	88
½ small banana, sliced	99
2 tablespoons sherbet	85
1 tablespoon cottage cheese	82
2 teaspoons maple syrup	88
1 teaspoon confectioner's sugar	78
1 tablespoon apple butter	92
1 teaspoon chopped peanuts	74

FRUIT COMPOTE

1 16-ounce can grapefruit
sections, drained

2 oranges, sectioned

1 cup pineapple sherbet
mint sprigs

Place chilled fruit in 8 individual dishes or serving bowl. Top with small scoops of sherbet and garnish with mint.

Serves 8 (68 calories each)

FRUIT MEDLEY

2 cups grapefruit sections
1 cup cantaloupe balls

1 cup blueberries

Combine and chill fruits. Serve in glass bowl.

Serves 4 (80 calories each)

GINGER MELON

1 honeydew melon
2 tablespoons lime juice

½ teaspoon powdered ginger

Cut honeydew melon into 6 wedges. Sprinkle wedges with lime juice and dust with powdered ginger. Serve ice cold.

Serves 6 (50 calories each)

GRAPEFRUIT BRULÉE

2 grapefruit
4 teaspoons brown sugar

⅛ teaspoon cinnamon
4 maraschino cherries

Cut grapefruit in half and cut around each section. Mix together sugar and cinnamon and sprinkle over grapefruit halves. Broil 5 minutes or until warm and bubbly. Top with cherry to serve.

Serves 4 (75 calories each)

MELON MIXUP

1 cup cantaloupe balls
1 cup honeydew balls
1 cup watermelon balls

½ cup lime juice
1 tablespoon sugar
crushed mint leaves

Combine all ingredients and chill thoroughly.

Serves 6 (45 calories each)

PEACHY DESSERT

4 fresh peaches   1 teaspoon cinnamon
4 teaspoons brown sugar

Skin, pit, and halve peaches. Sprinkle with brown sugar and cinnamon. Bake at 300° for 10 minutes, then put under broiler for a few minutes to brown slightly.

Serves 4 (55 calories each)

PEARS POACHED IN WINE

¾ cup water   1 cinnamon stick
¼ cup red wine   4 whole pears, peeled
1 small piece lemon rind

Combine water, wine, lemon rind, and cinnamon stick. Bring to a boil. Drop in whole fruit and simmer until soft. Serve well chilled.

Serves 4 (100 calories each)

PINEAPPLE FRAPPÉ

2 cups ripe fresh pineapple   few mint leaves
1 cup crushed ice

Combine all ingredients in blender at highest speed. Serve in well-chilled glasses.

Serves 6 (23 calories each)

PINEAPPLE STRAWBERRY COMPOTE

1½ cups fresh pineapple   1 pint hulled strawberries
      chunks

Combine fruits and toss together when ready to serve.
Serves 6 (60 calories each)

SOUTHERN AMBROSIA

1 16-ounce can grapefruit   2 oranges, sectioned
   sections, drained   1 banana, sliced
4 tablespoons shredded
   coconut

Place half the grapefruit sections in serving bowl. Sprinkle lightly with 1 tablespoon coconut. Add a layer of
orange sections, then banana; sprinkle with 2 tablespoons coconut. Top with remaining grapefruit and coconut. Chill at least one hour before serving.
Serves 6 (80 calories each)

SPANISH CREAM

1 envelope unflavored   2 eggs, separated
   gelatin   2 cups skim milk
2 tablespoons sugar   1 teaspoon vanilla
⅛ teaspoon salt   ½ cup strawberries

Mix together gelatin, sugar, and salt in top of double boiler. Beat together egg yolks and milk. Add to gelatin mixture. Place over boiling water and stir constantly until gelatin is thoroughly dissolved, about 5 minutes. Remove from heat and stir in vanilla. Chill until mixture mounds slightly when dropped from a spoon. Beat egg whites until foamy; gradually beat in 1 more tablespoon sugar and beat until stiff. Fold into gelatin mixture. Turn into 4-cup glass bowl and chill until firm. Decorate with fresh or frozen strawberries.

Serves 6 (80 calories each)

SPICED CRANSHAW MELON

1 large cranshaw melon
½ cup fresh lime juice
3 tablespoons honey

1 teaspoon ground coriander

Chill melon. Combine lime juice, honey, and coriander; cover and chill for several hours. To serve, slice melon into thin lengthwise crescents and cut off rind. Spoon dressing over each piece of melon.

Serves 8 (75 calories each)

STEWED APPLES

4 apples
1 teaspoon cinnamon
1 tablespoon lemon juice

1 tablespoon sugar
few drops red food coloring

Pare apples, core, and quarter. Drop apples into ½ cup water with remaining ingredients. Simmer 3 minutes.

Serves 8 (40 calories each)

STRAWBERRY YOGURT DESSERT

1 cup plain yogurt
½ cup strawberries
1½ teaspoons sugar

1 teaspoon vanilla
½ teaspoon cinnamon

Combine and chill.

Serves 2 (85 calories each)

SUMMER COOLER

2 cups watermelon balls
1½ cups fresh pineapple
chunks

mint leaves

Combine fruits and garnish with mint leaves. Serve icy cold.

Serves 6 (50 calories each)

YOGURT FLIP

1 envelope unflavored
  gelatin
1 tablespoon lemon juice
2 tablespoons water

1 cup strawberries
1 cup crushed pineapple
1 cup plain yogurt

In top of double boiler over hot water combine and soften gelatin, lemon juice, and water. Add fruits and yogurt. Whip until fluffy. Spoon into individual dishes. Chill until firm.

Serves 4 (70 calories each)

Sensible Substitutions

For This	Calories	Substitute This	Calories	Calories Saved
Milk, 8 ounces	160	Skim milk, 8 ounces	90	70
Prune juice, 8 ounces	200	Tomato juice, 8 ounces	45	155
Coffee with cream and sugar	95	Black coffee	0	95
Orange juice, 8 ounces	110	Vegetable juice cocktail, 8 ounces	40	70
Chocolate malted, 8 ounces	450	Tea, unsweetened	0	450
Scrambled eggs, 2	220	Boiled or poached eggs, 2	160	60
Cream cheese, 1 ounce	105	Low-fat cottage cheese, 1 ounce	20	85
Cheese cake, 2-inch piece	200	1/2 cantaloupe	60	140
Apple pie, 1 slice	345	Tangerine, 1	40	305
Peach pie, 1 slice	280	Peach, 1	35	245
Chocolate cake, 2-inch piece	445	Grapefruit, 1/2	55	390
Ice cream cone	210	Banana, 1	85	125
Tuna fish, 3 ounces	170	Crabmeat, 3 ounces	85	85
Duck, 4 ounces	200	Chicken, 4 ounces	140	60
Pork chop, 3 ounces	340	Veal chop, 3 ounces	185	155
Hamburger, 4 ounces	320	Lamb chop, 4 ounces	140	180
Steak, 4 ounces	300	Red snapper, 4 ounces	105	195
Peanuts, 1 ounce	190	Apple, 1	70	120
Peanuts, 1 cup	800	Grapes, 1 cup	65	735
Bean soup, 1 cup	170	Beef bouillon, 1 cup	30	140
Baked beans, 1 cup	320	Green beans, 1 cup	30	290
Lima beans, 1 cup	180	Asparagus, 1 cup	35	145
Winter squash, 1 cup	130	Summer squash, 1 cup	30	100
Succotash, 1 cup	260	Spinach, 1 cup	40	220
Beer, 8 ounces	105	Club soda, 8 ounces	0	105

CALORIE COUNTDOWN

	Calories
Apple juice, ½ cup	60
Apples	
fresh, ½ pound	120
fresh, 1 average	70
Apricots, fresh, ½ pound	110
Artichoke hearts, frozen, 3	20
Asparagus, cooked, 6 spears	20
Bananas, fresh, 1 average	85
Bean sprouts, ½ cup	15

  * These figures are from Bernice K. Watt and Annabel L. Merrill, *Composition of Foods: Raw, Processed, Prepared*, U.S. Dept. of Agriculture Handbook No. 8 (revised, December 1963).

	Calories
Beans, green, ½ cup	15
Beans, wax, ½ cup	20
Beef	
flank steak, 4 ounces	225
ground, lean, broiled, 4 ounces	250
lean cuts, braised, simmered, or pot roasted, 4 ounces	225
porterhouse steak, lean, broiled, 4 ounces	255
round steak, lean, broiled, 4 ounces	220
Beef broth, bouillon, consommé, ½ cup	15
Beet greens, boiled, ½ cup	12
Blueberries, ½ cup	40
Bluefish, 4 ounces	130
Broccoli, cooked, ½ cup	20
Brussels sprouts, cooked, ½ cup	25
Butter, salted or unsalted	
½ cup or ¼ pound	800
1 tablespoon	100
Buttermilk, 8 ounces	90
Cabbage, Chinese, raw, ½ cup	5
Cabbage, raw, shredded, ½ cup	8
Cantaloupe, fresh	
½ melon	60
diced, ½ cup	35
Carrots	
raw, grated, ½ cup	22
raw, 1 average	20
boiled, diced, ½ cup	25
Casaba melon, fresh, ½ pound	30
Catsup (or chili sauce), 1 tablespoon	15
Cauliflower	
raw, ½ pound	60
boiled, ½ cup	15
Caviar, 1 ounce	75
Celery	
raw, 1 stalk	5

	Calories
raw, diced, 1/2 cup	8
boiled, 1/2 cup	10
Cheese	
American, 1 ounce	105
blue or roquefort, 1 ounce	103
cheddar, 1 ounce	111
cheddar or American, grated, 1 tablespoon	30
cottage, 1 percent butterfat, 1/2 cup	75
cream, 1 ounce	105
Parmesan, grated, 1 tablespoon	25
Cherries, sweet, fresh, 1/2 cup	40
Cherries, maraschino, 1 average	10
Chicken	
broiled, meat only, 4 ounces	155
roasted, 4 ounces	210
broth, 1/2 cup	20
liver, 4 ounces	145
Clam-tomato juice, 4 ounces	20
Clams, canned, 4 ounces	60
Cornstarch, 1 tablespoon	30
Crabmeat, 4 ounces	110
Cucumber, peeled, 1 average	30
Eggplant, cooked, 1 average	40
Eggs	
raw, whole, 1 large	80
raw, white	15
raw, yolk	60
Flounder, 4 ounces	85
Flour	
unsifted, 1/2 cup	225
1 tablespoon	25
Gelatin, unflavored, 1 tablespoon or 1 envelope	25
Ginger ale, 1/2 cup	35
Grapefruit, 1/2 average	55
Grapes, seedless, 1/2 cup	45

	Calories
Halibut, 4 ounces	110
Honey, 1 tablespoon	65
Honeydew melon	
1 wedge	50
½ cup, diced	40
Horseradish, prepared, 1 ounce	10
Lamb	
chop, broiled, 4 ounces	140
leg, roasted, 4 ounces	210
Lemon juice	
fresh, ½ cup	30
fresh, 1 tablespoon	4
Lemons, fresh, 1	20
Lettuce	
Boston or bibb, 1 head	30
iceberg, 1 head	60
Lime juice	
fresh, ½ cup	30
fresh, 1 tablespoon	4
Limes, fresh, 1 average	20
Lobster meat, 4 ounces	100
Mayonnaise, 1 tablespoon	65
Milk	
skim or buttermilk, 8 ounces	90
instant, nonfat dry, 8 ounces	245
Mushrooms	
raw, ½ pound	60
canned, with liquid, 4 ounces	20
Mustard, prepared, 1 ounce	25
Nectarines, fresh, 1 average	30
Oil, corn, olive, safflower, peanut, etc. (1 tablespoon)	125
Olives, 3 large green or 3 small black	15
Onions, raw	
1 average	40
chopped, 1 tablespoon	4

	Calories
Onions, green, raw, 3 small	10
Orange juice, fresh, 8 ounces	110
Oranges, 1 average	65
Parsley, raw, chopped, 1 tablespoon	2
Peaches, fresh, 1 average	35
Pears, fresh, 1 average	100
Peas, boiled, ½ cup	55
Peapods, 8 ounces	115
Peppers, sweet, green, raw, 1 average	15
Pickles, dill, 4 ounces	12
Pimientos, canned, 4 ounces	30
Pineapple	
fresh, 1 slice	45
fresh, diced, ½ cup	35
crushed, canned in own juice, 8 ounces	125
Radishes, raw, 4 small	5
Raisins, ½ cup	240
Raspberries, ½ cup	35
Red snapper, raw, 4 ounces	105
Rice, white, cooked, ½ cup	90
Salmon	
fresh, 8 ounces	320
canned, 4 ounces	160
Sauces	
hot pepper, 1 teaspoon	1
soy, 1 tablespoon	9
tomato, canned, ½ cup	35
Worcestershire, 1 tablespoon	15
Scallops, 8 ounces	185
Shrimp, cleaned, 8 ounces	210
Sole, fillet of, 8 ounces	175
Spinach	
raw, ½ pound	60
boiled, ½ cup	20
Squash, summer, cooked, ½ cup	15

	Calories
Strawberries, fresh, ½ cup	25
Sugar	
brown, 1 cup	820
brown, 1 tablespoon	50
white, 1 cup	770
white, 1 tablespoon	40
Tomatoes	
canned, with liquid, ½ cup	25
fresh, ½ pound	50
fresh, 1 average	20
juice, 8 ounces	45
paste, 4 ounces	90
sauce, canned, ½ cup	35
Tongue, beef, braised, 4 ounces	275
Tuna, canned	
in oil, drained, 4 ounces	225
in water, 4 ounces	145
Turkey, roasted, 4 ounces	210
Veal	
cutlet, 4 ounces	230
loin, broiled, 4 ounces	265
Vegetable juice cocktail, 8 ounces	40
Vinegar, 1 tablespoon	2
Water chestnuts, 4 ounces	65
Watermelon	
fresh, 1 wedge	115
fresh, cubes, ½ cup	25
Wine	
red, 1 cup after cooking	29
white, 1 cup after cooking	26
sherry, 1 cup after cooking	48
sherry, 1 tablespoon after cooking	6
Yogurt, plain, made from skim milk, 8 ounces	125

INDEX